DOG FACE
COLORING BOOK

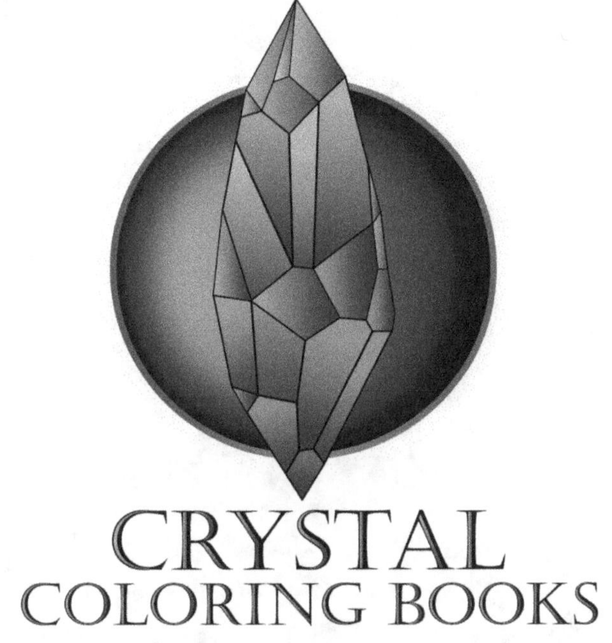

CRYSTAL
COLORING BOOKS

ISBN: 9781719965552

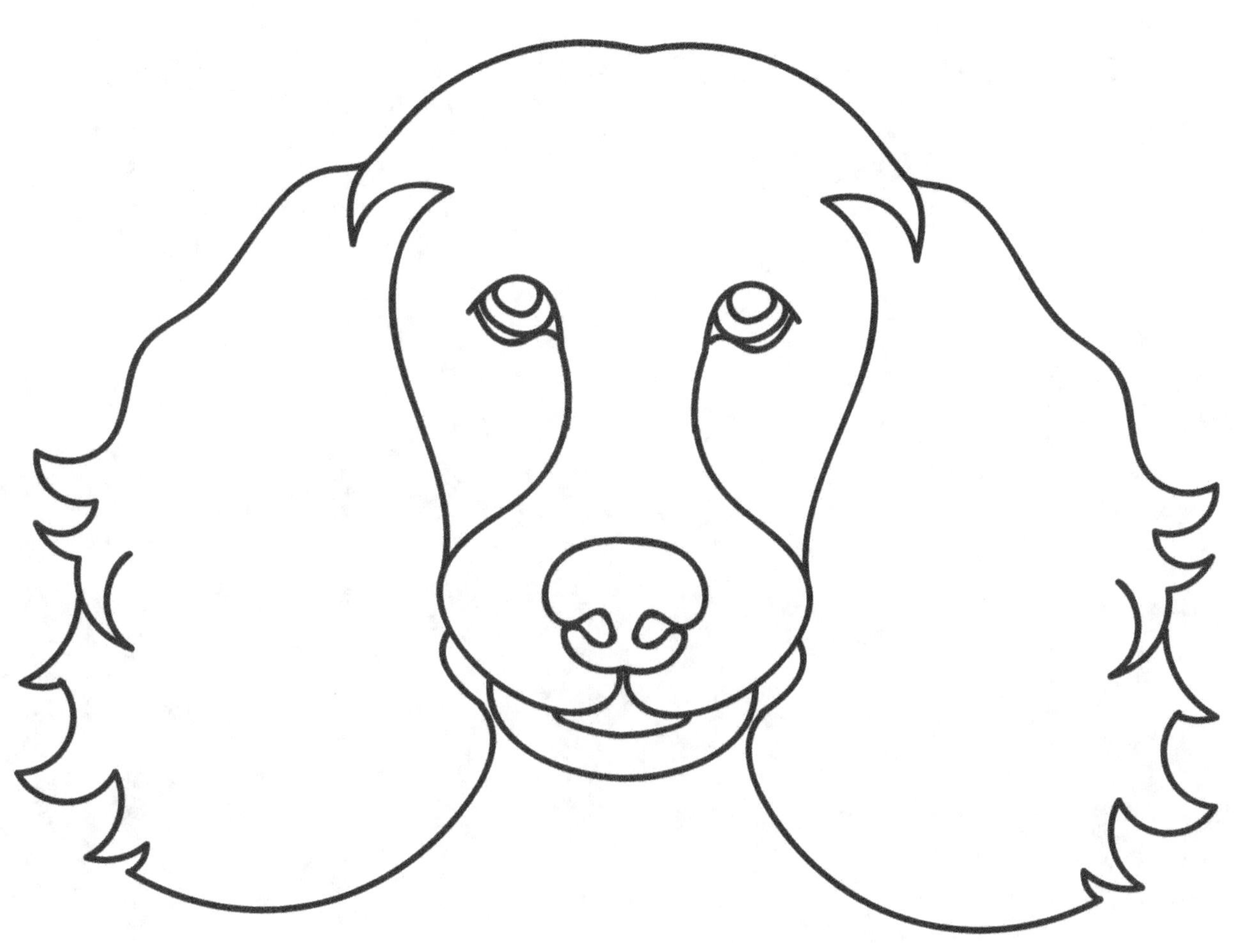

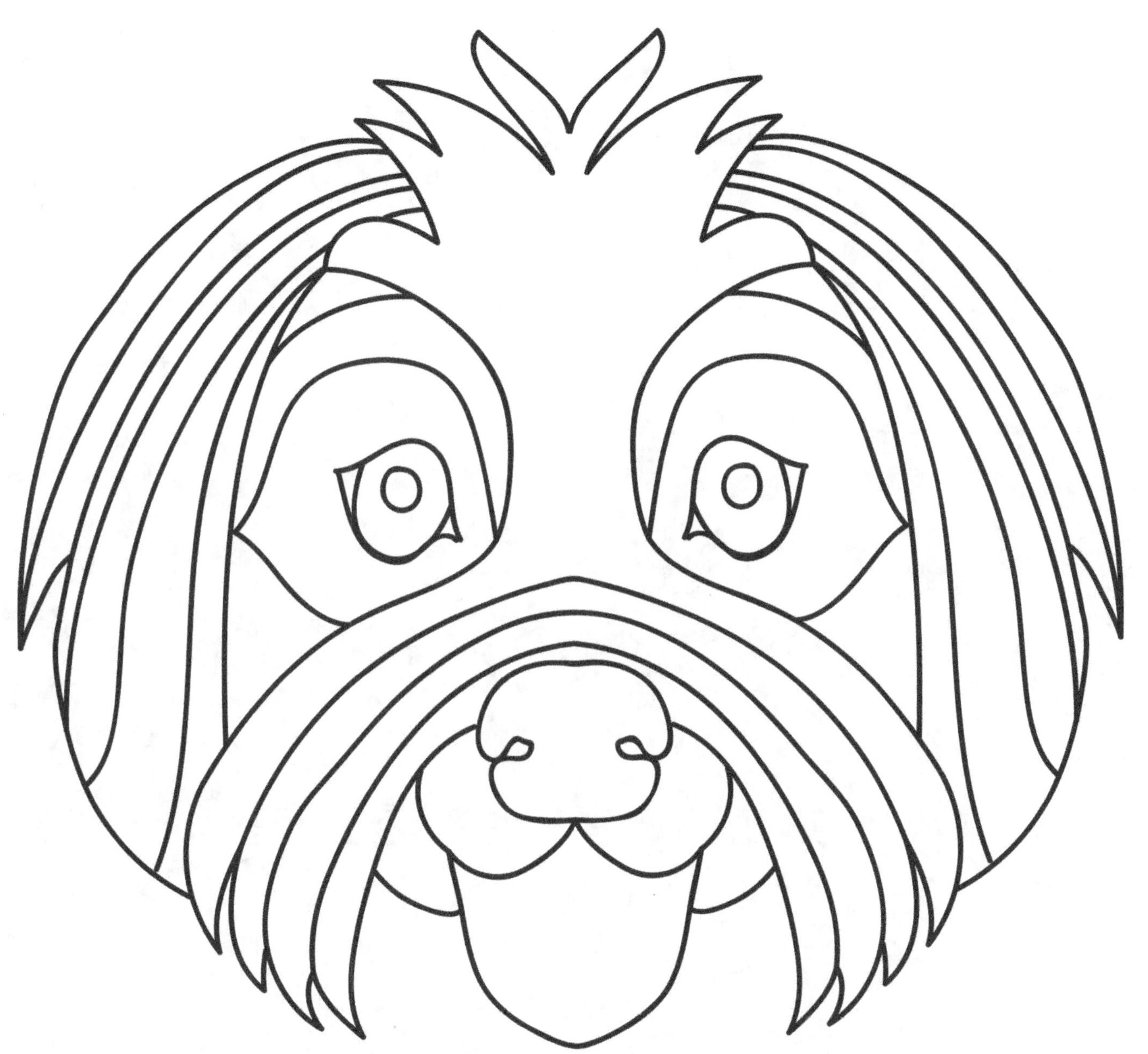

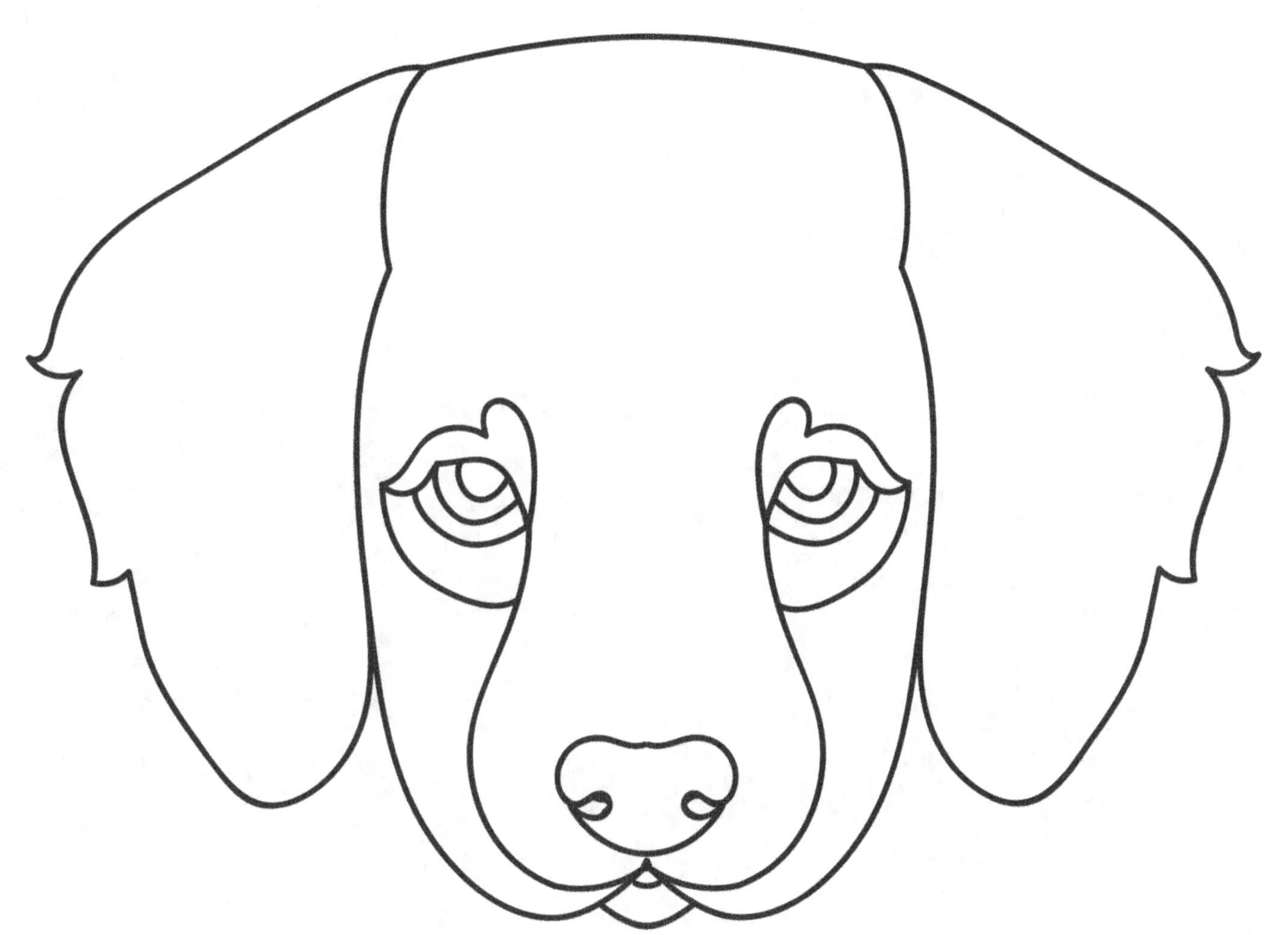

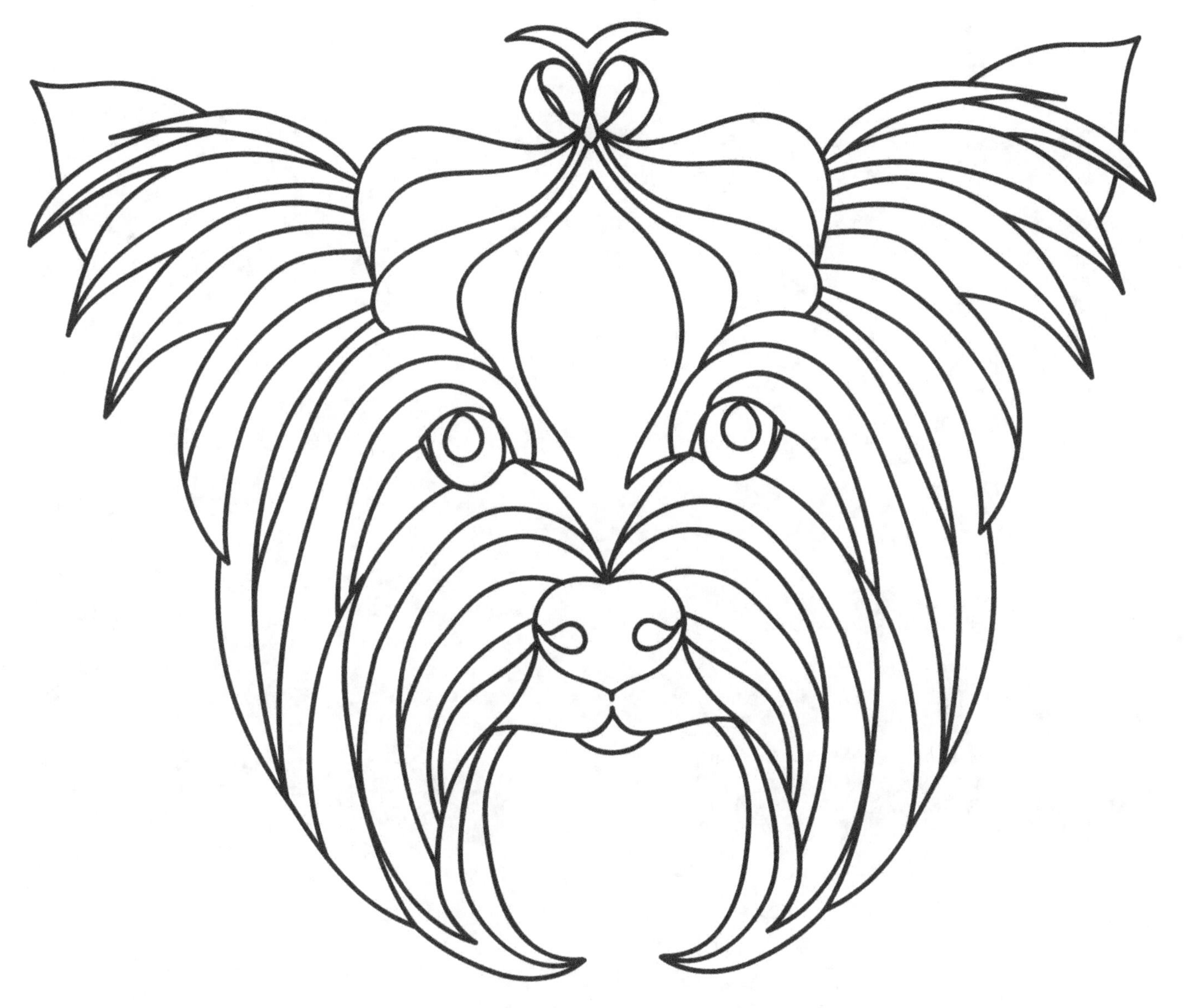

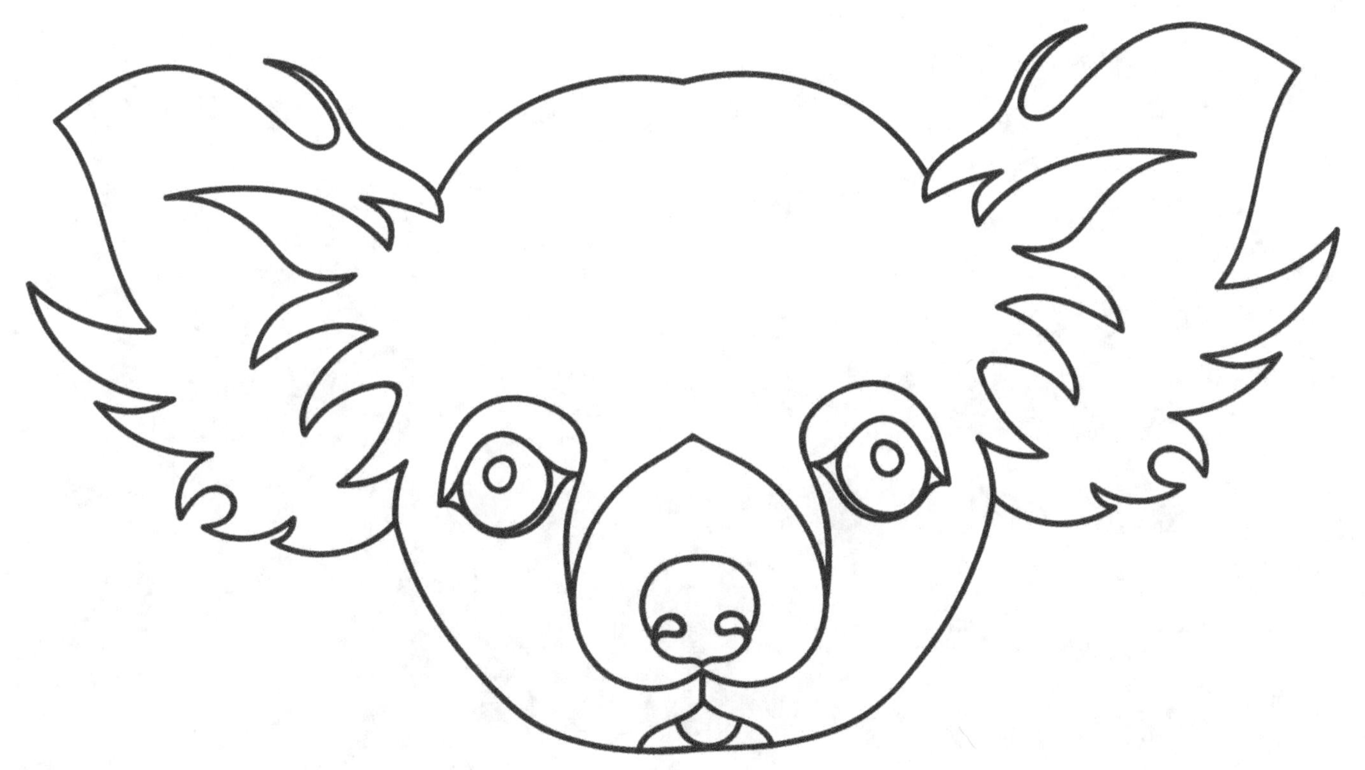

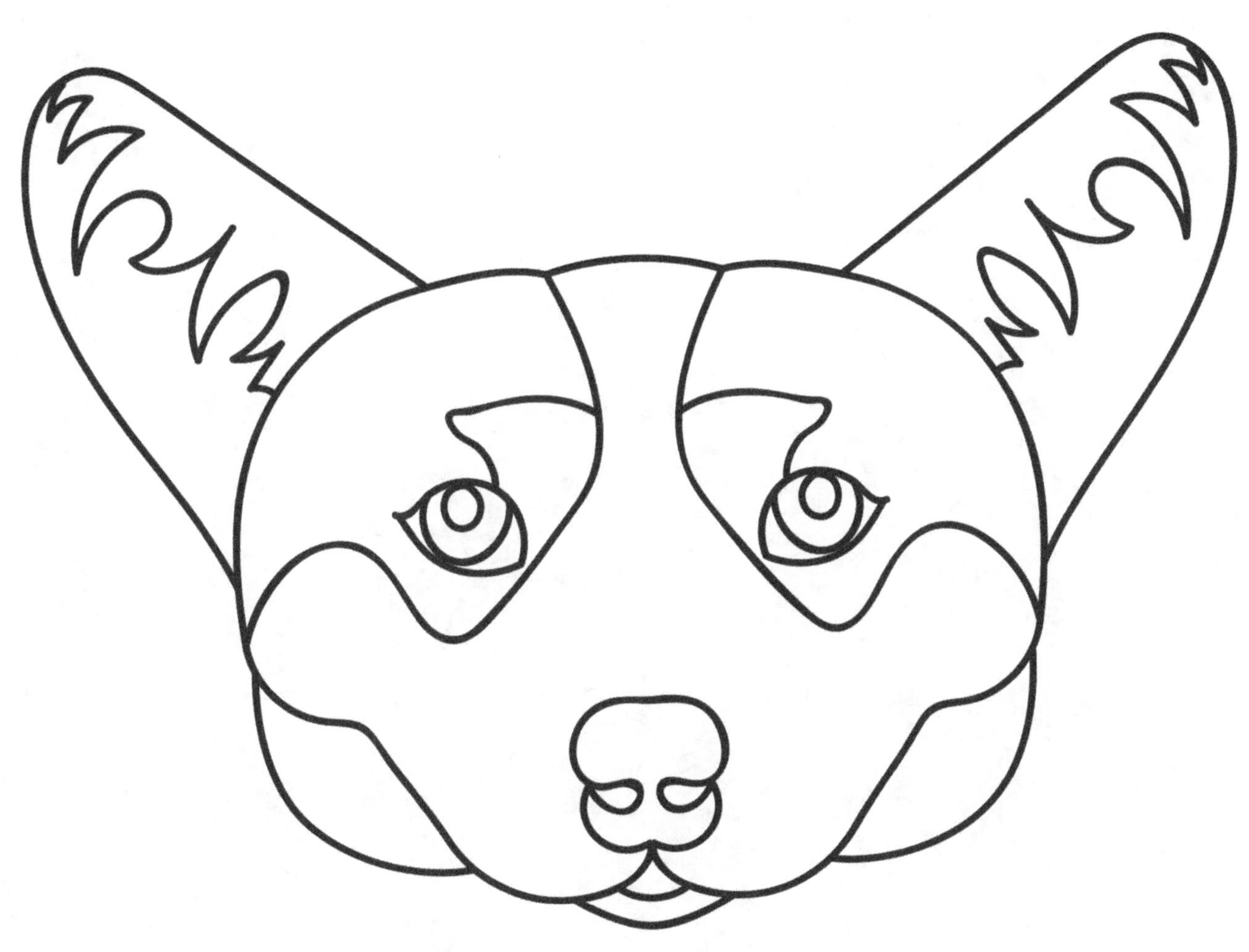

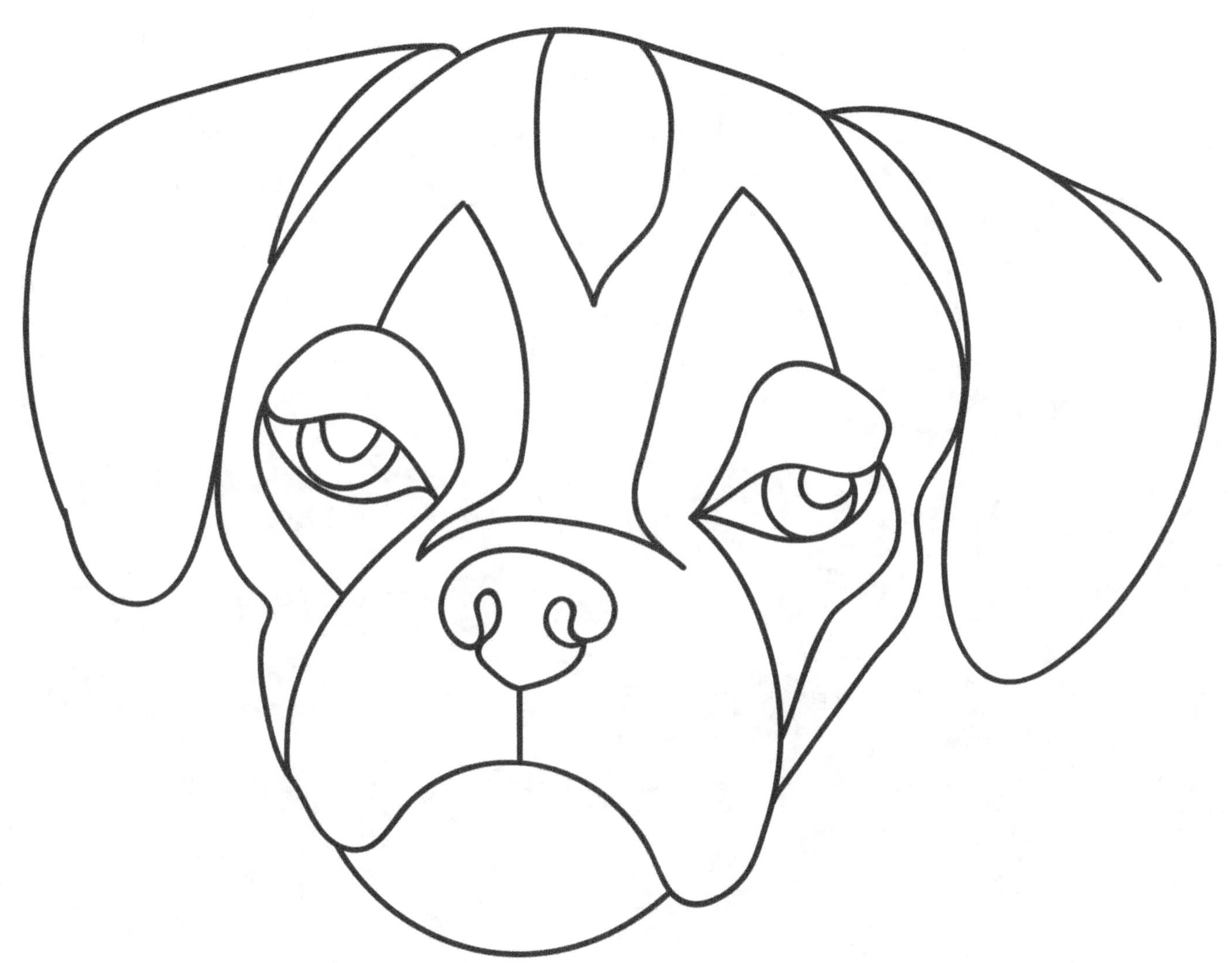

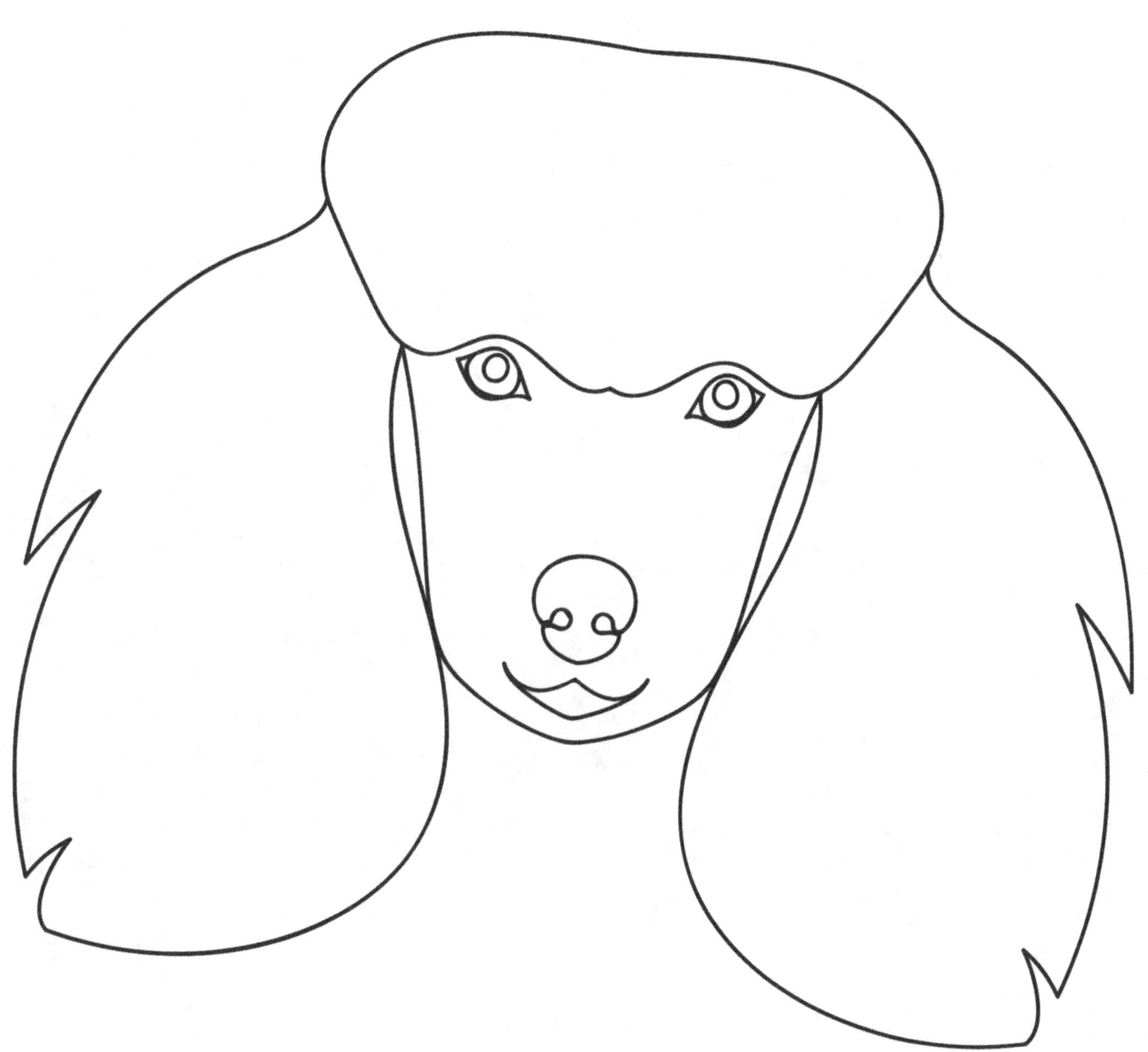

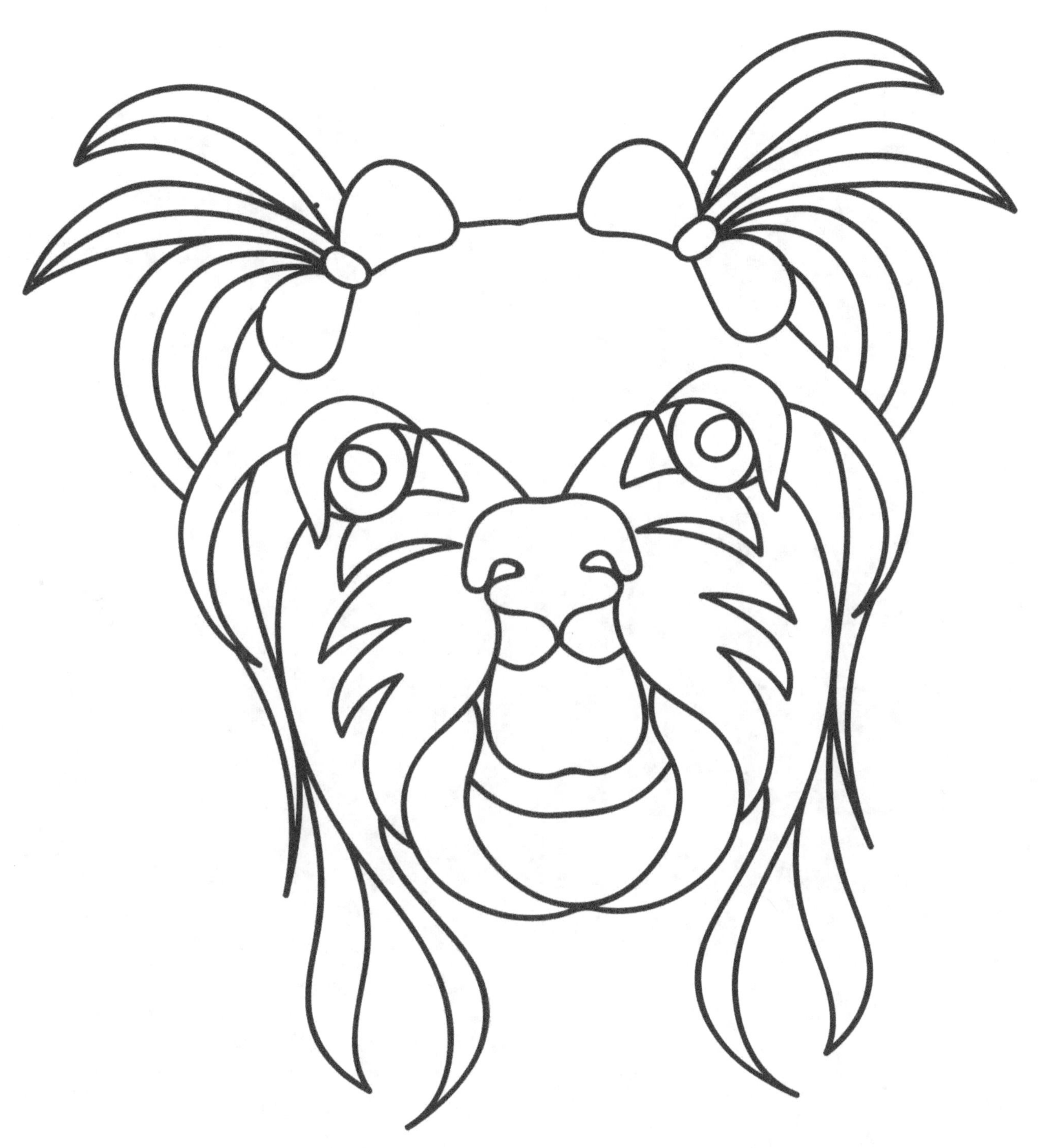

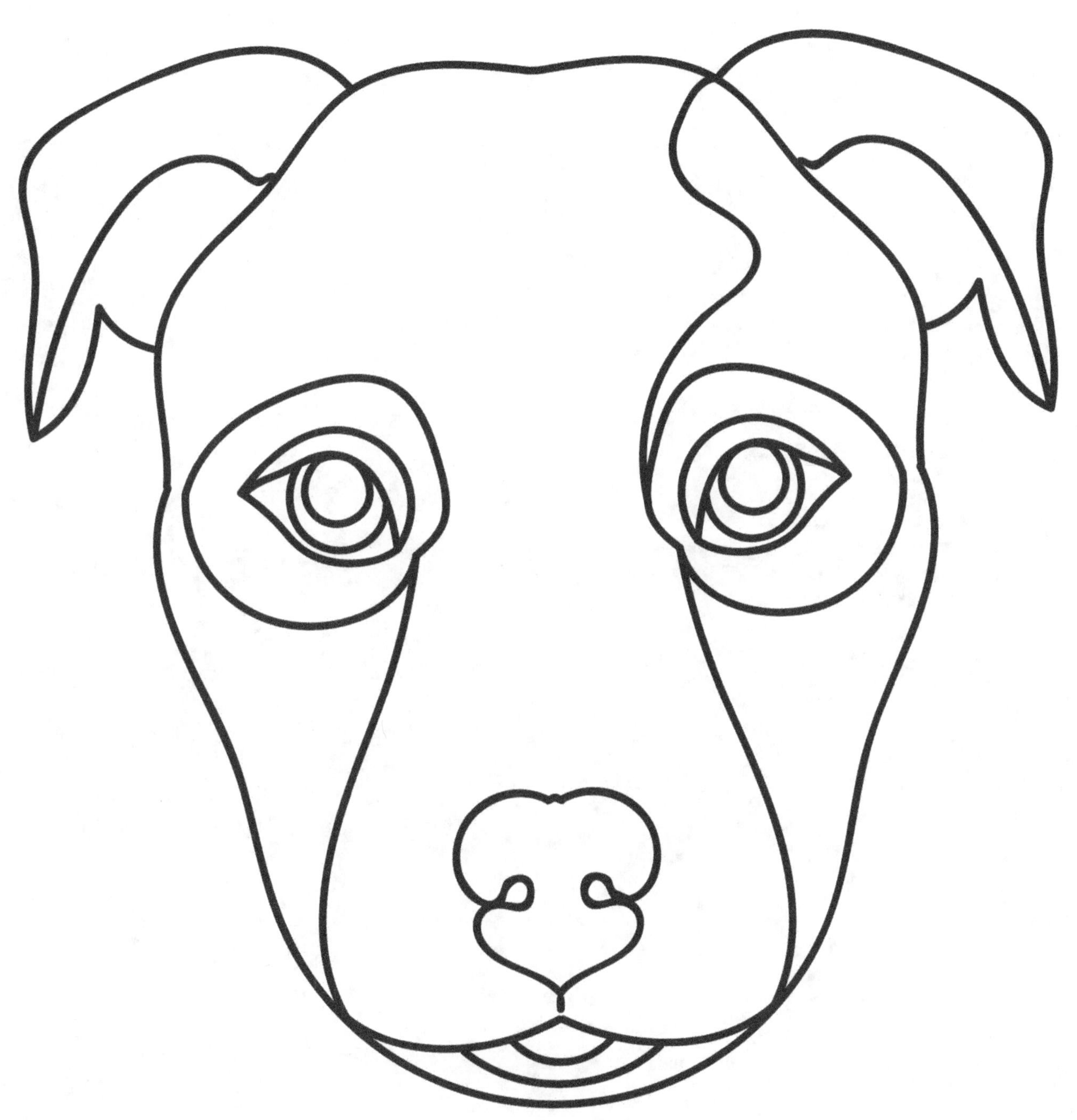

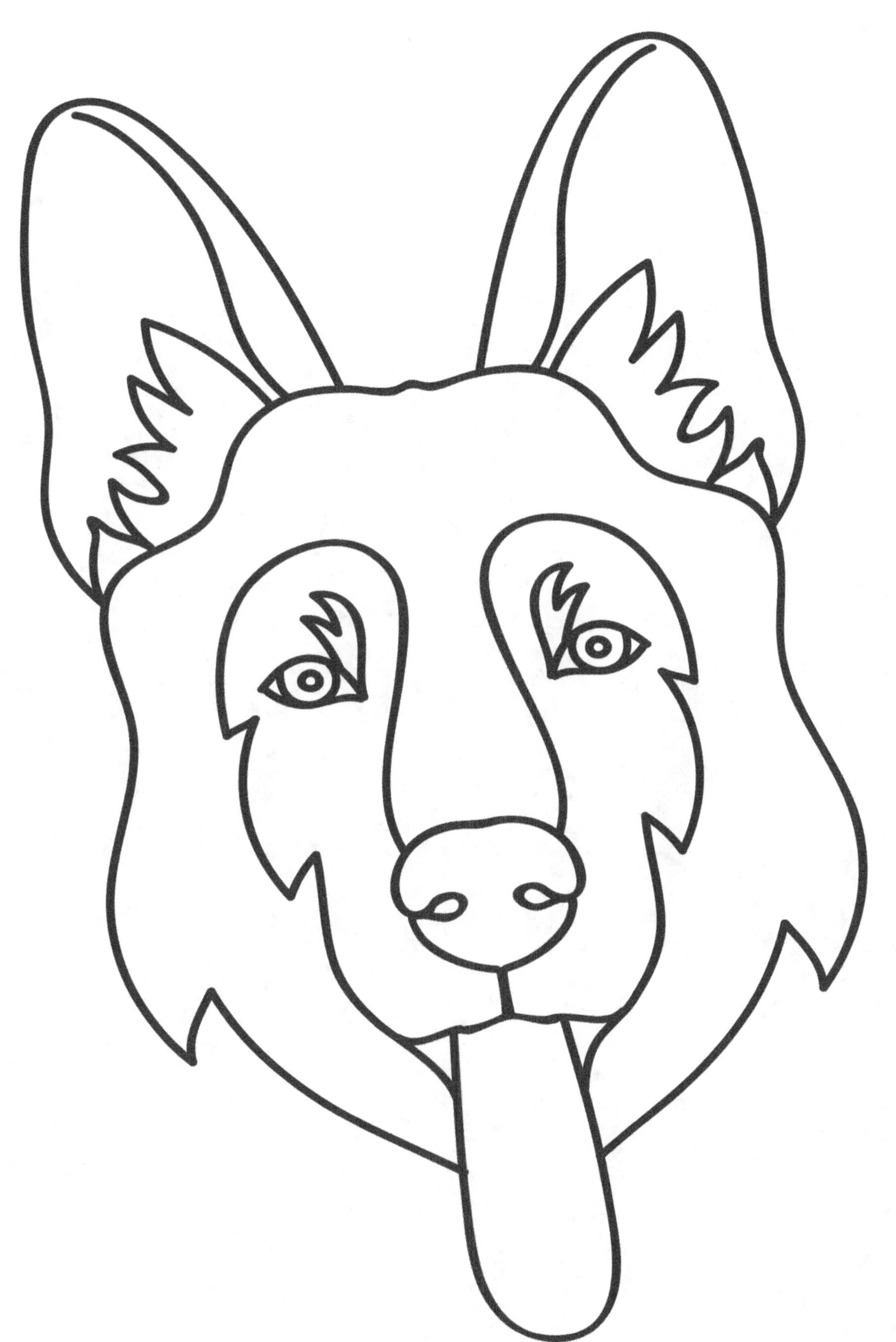

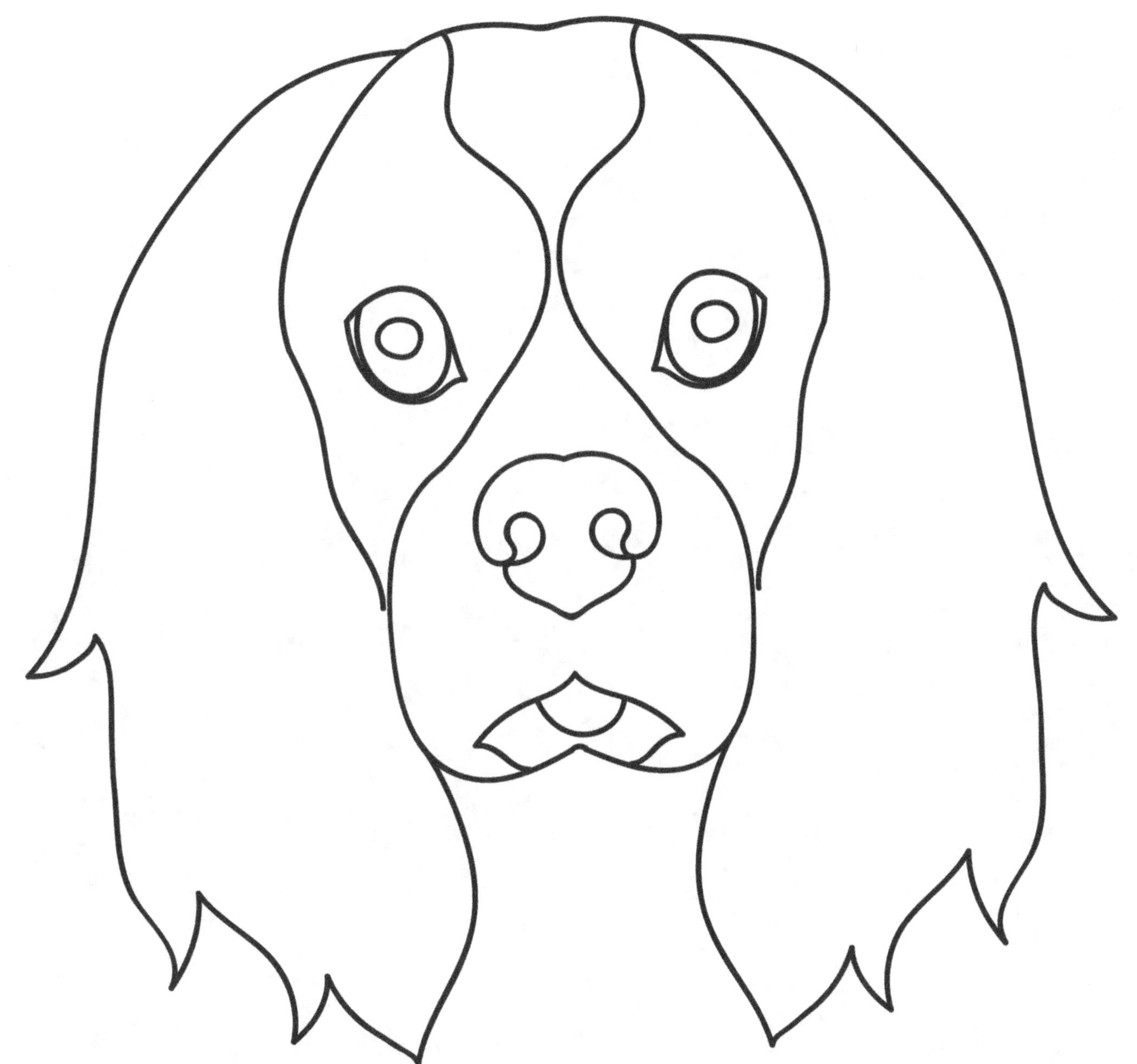

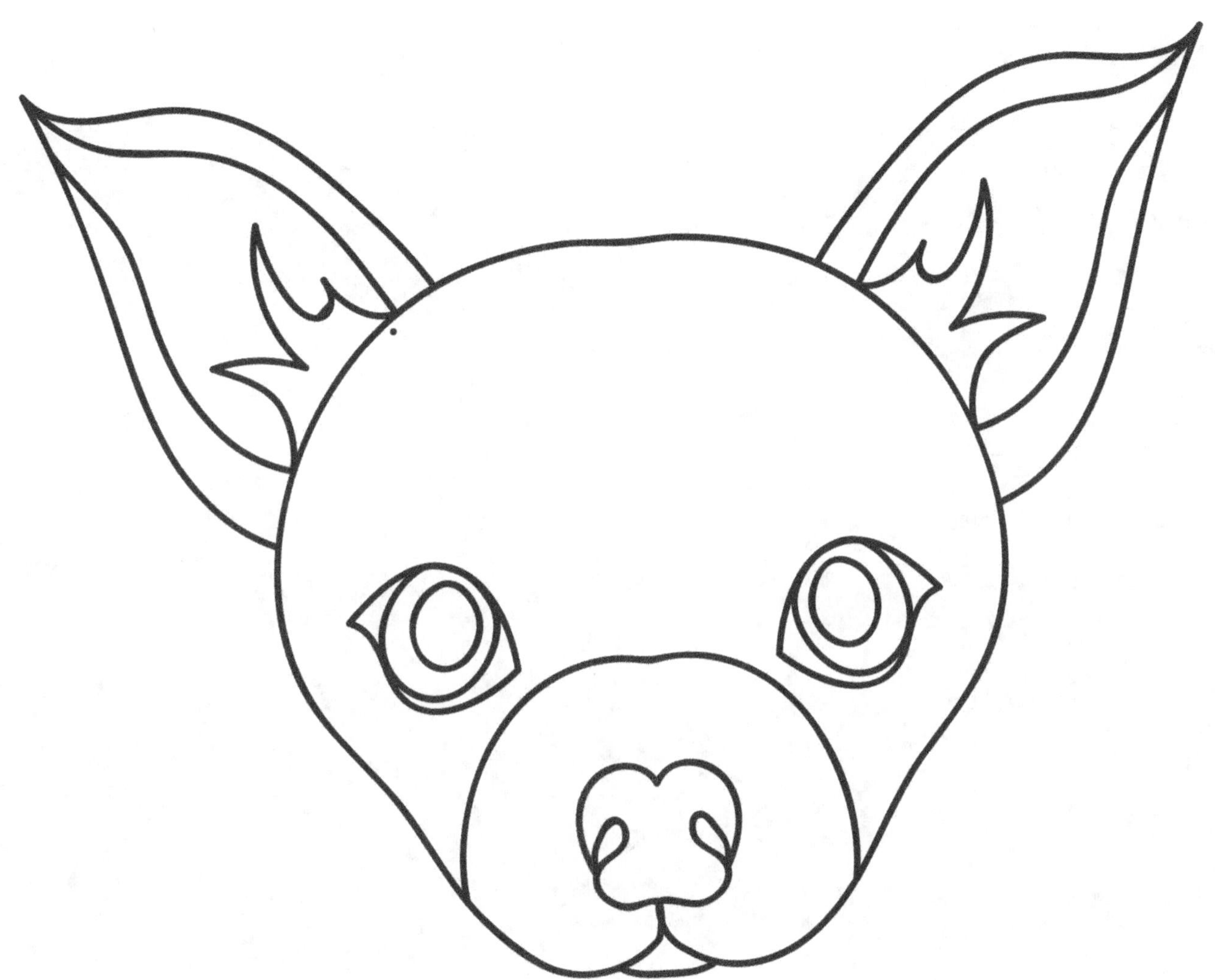

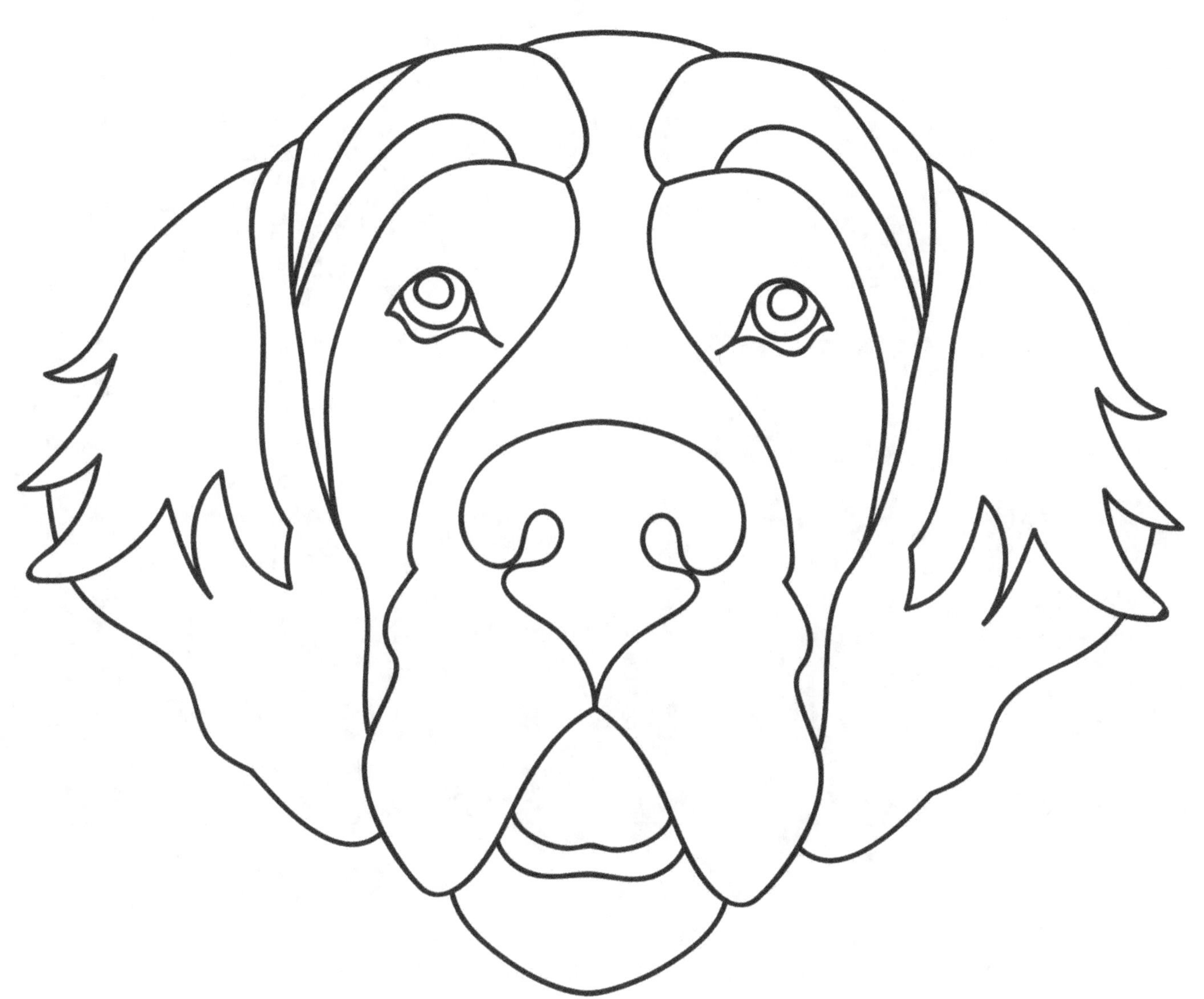

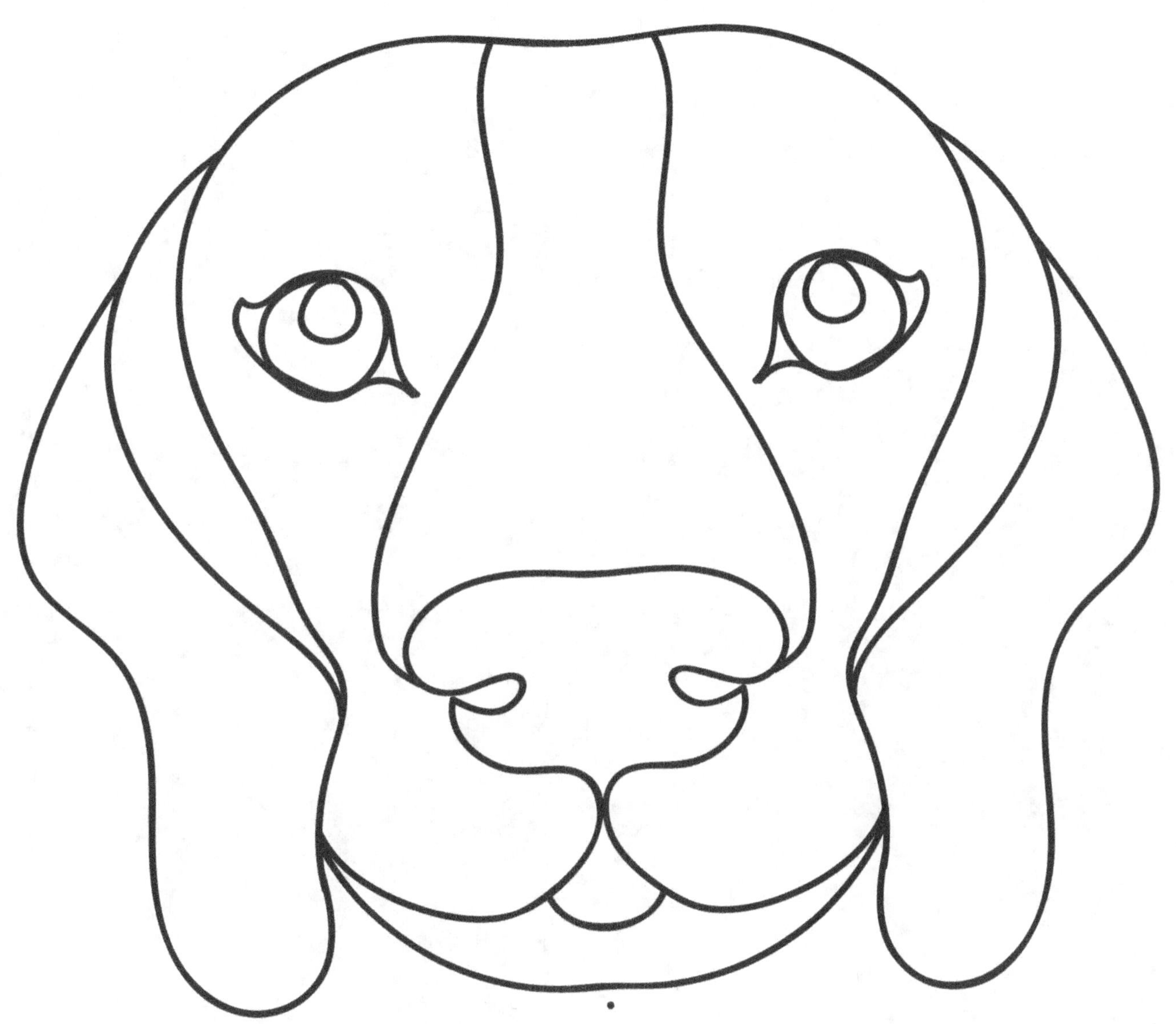

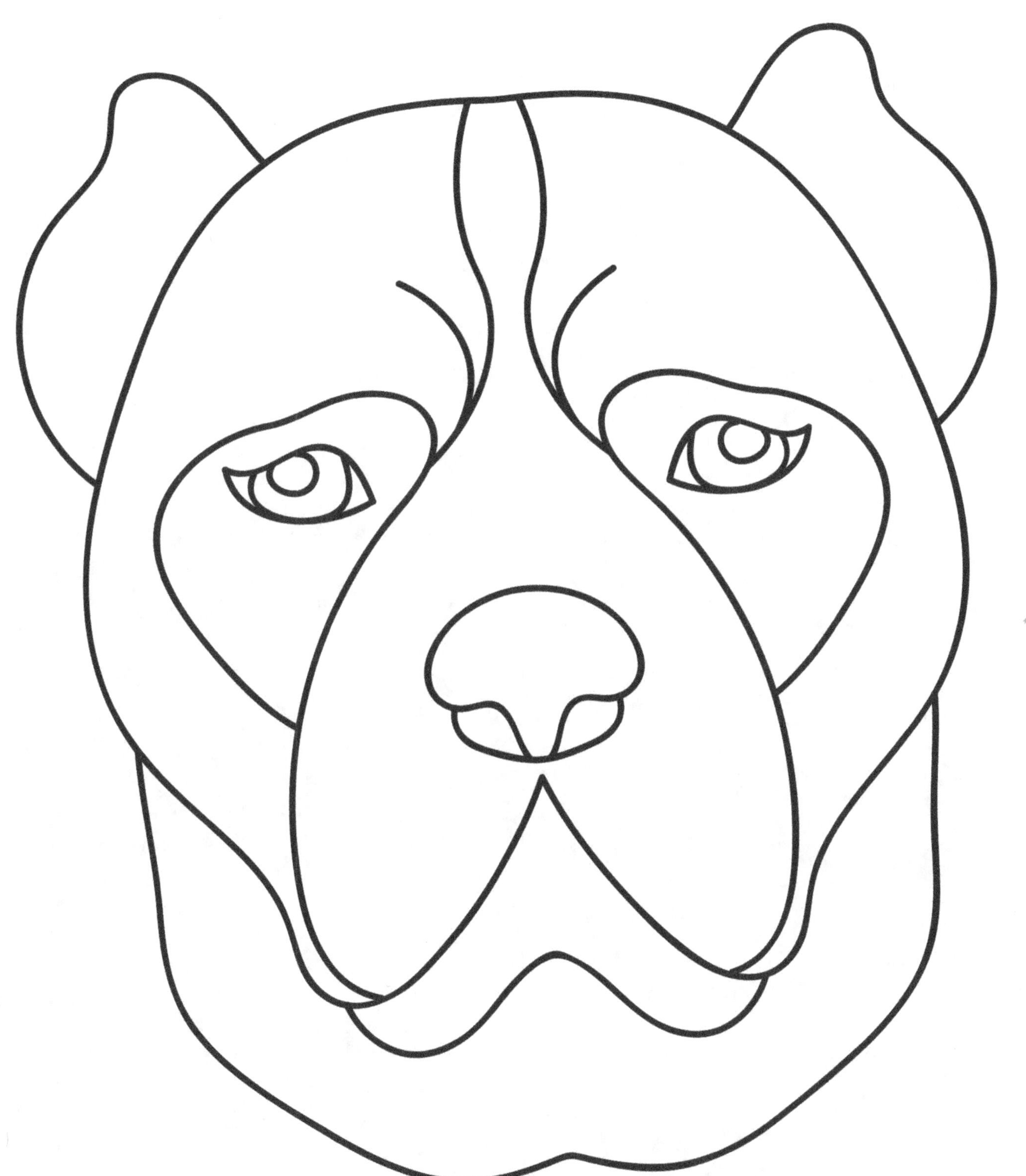

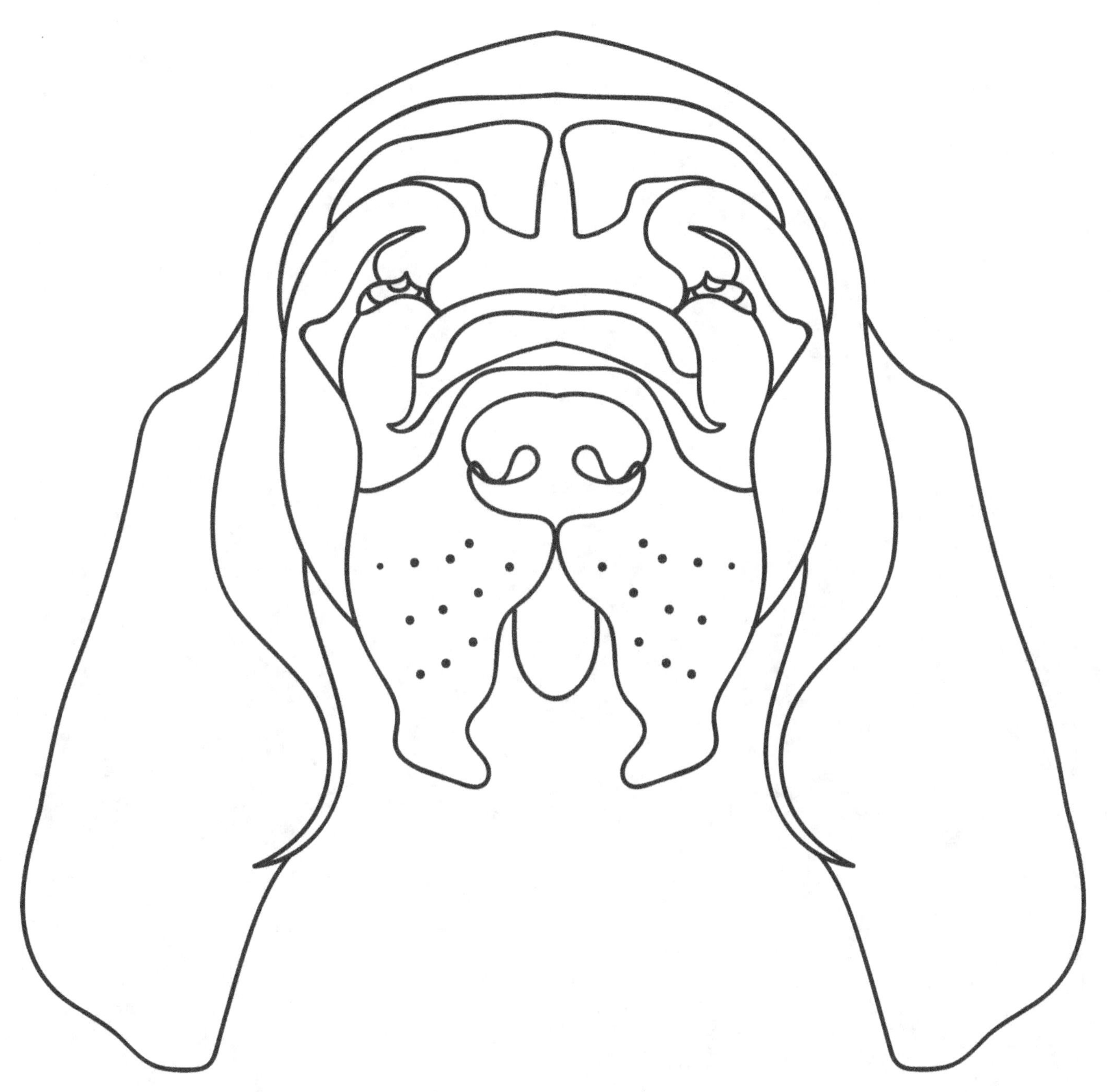

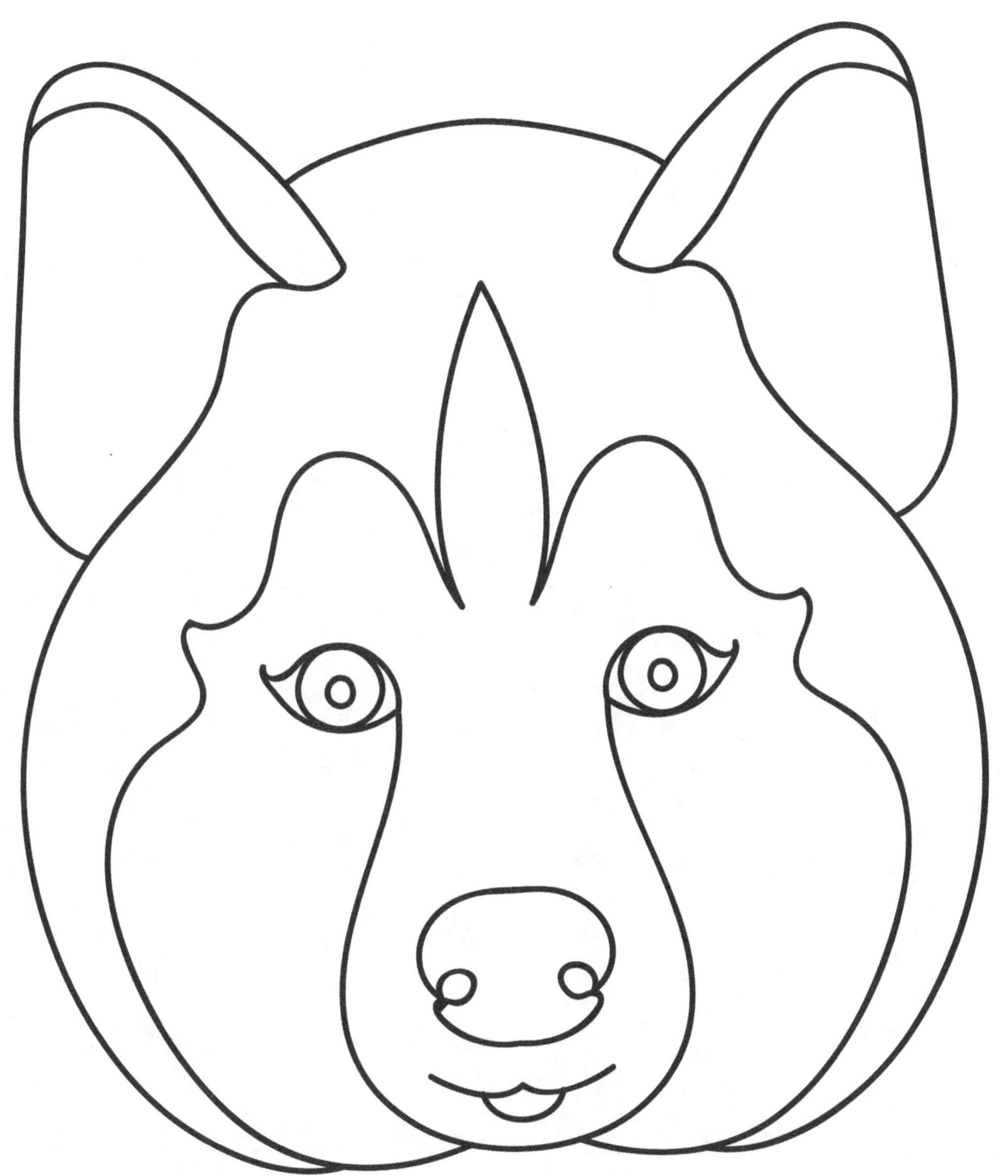

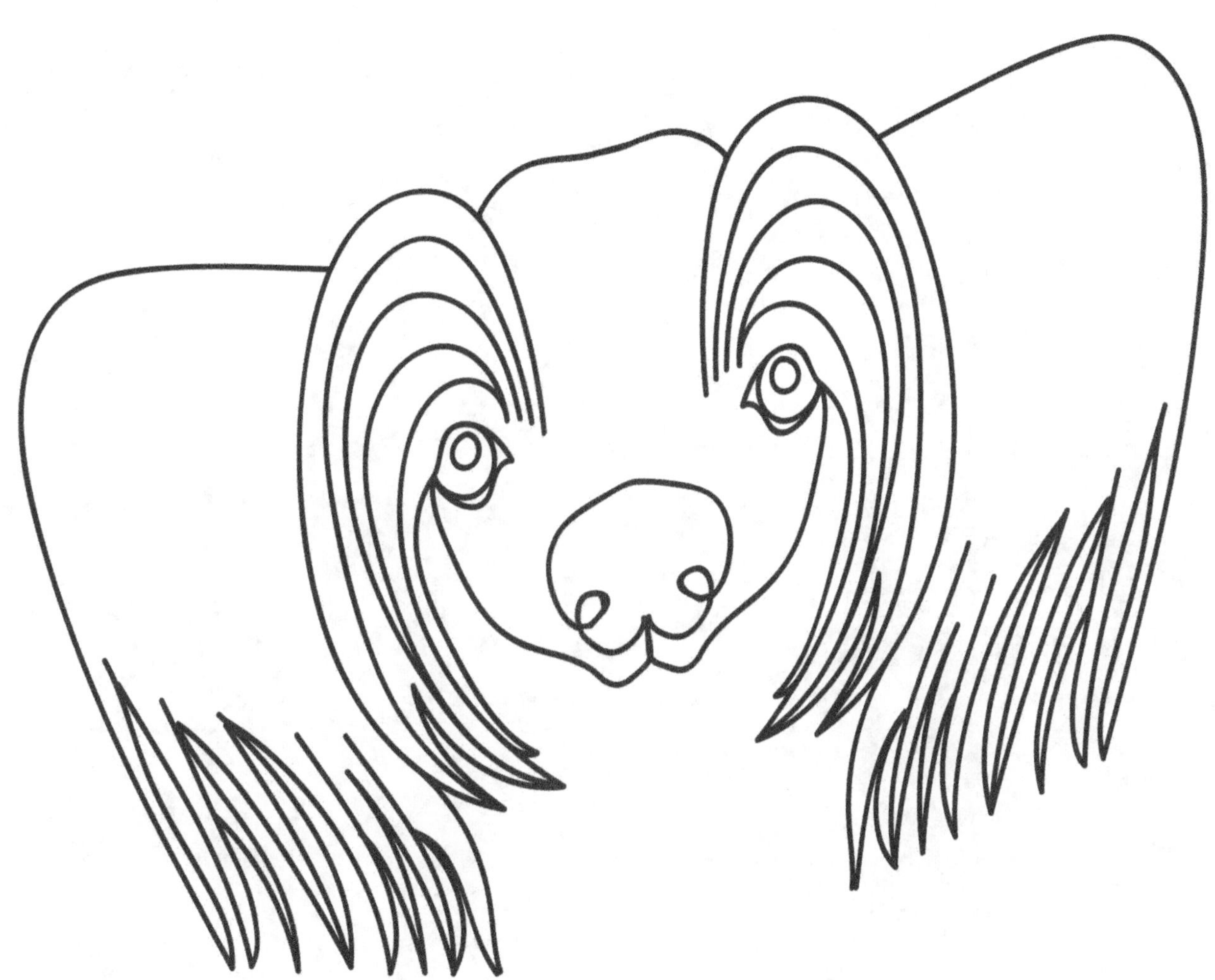

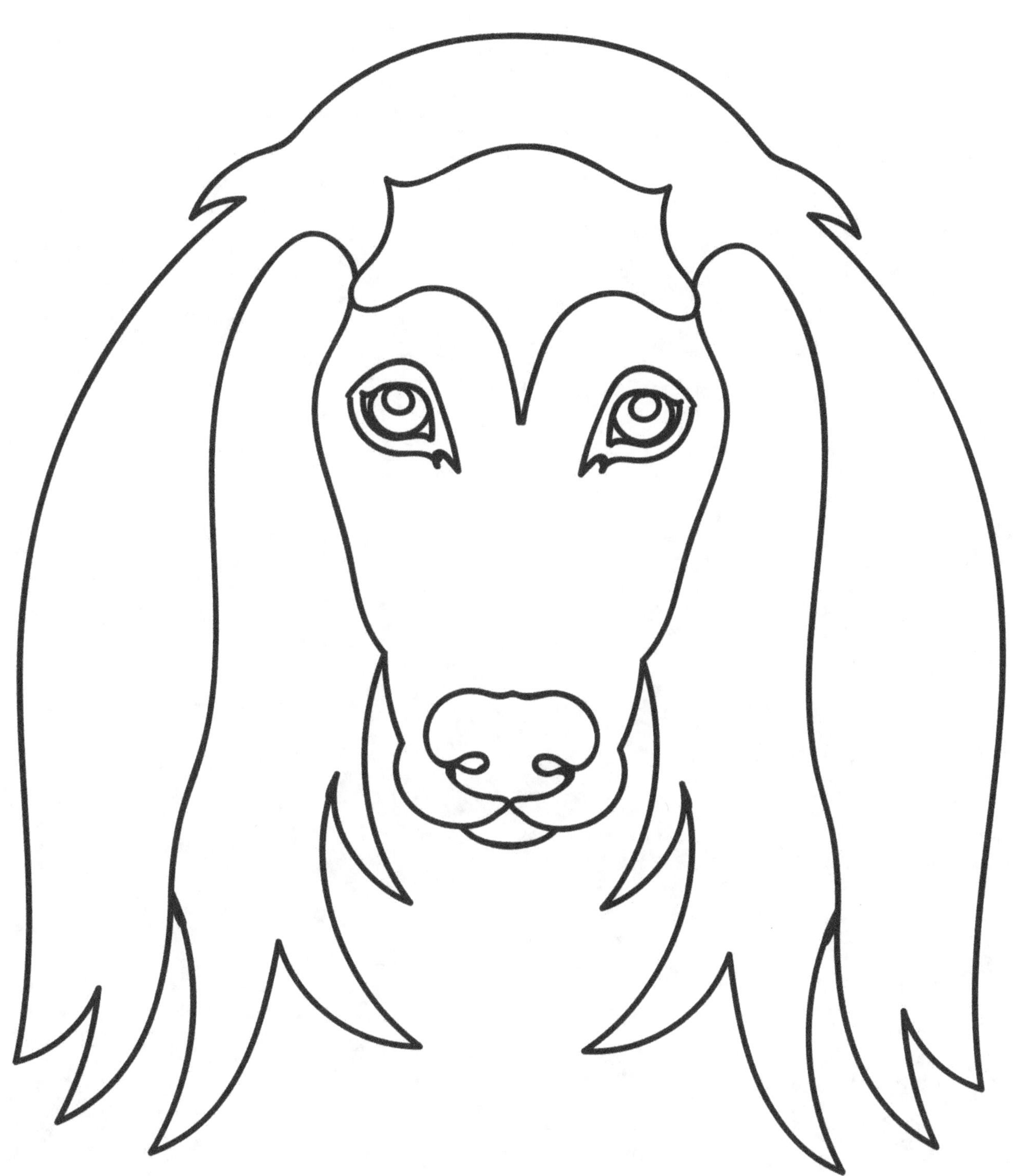

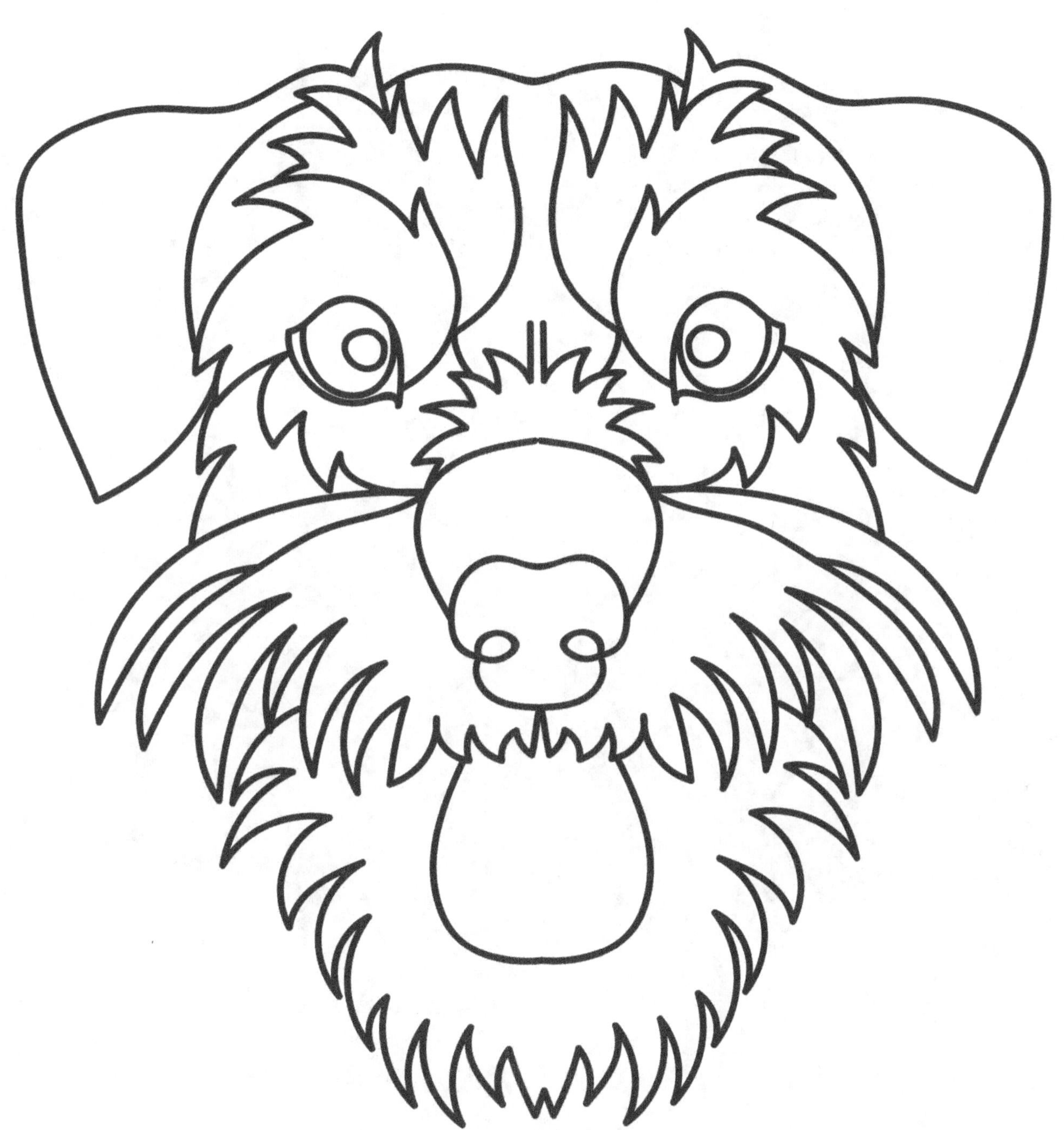

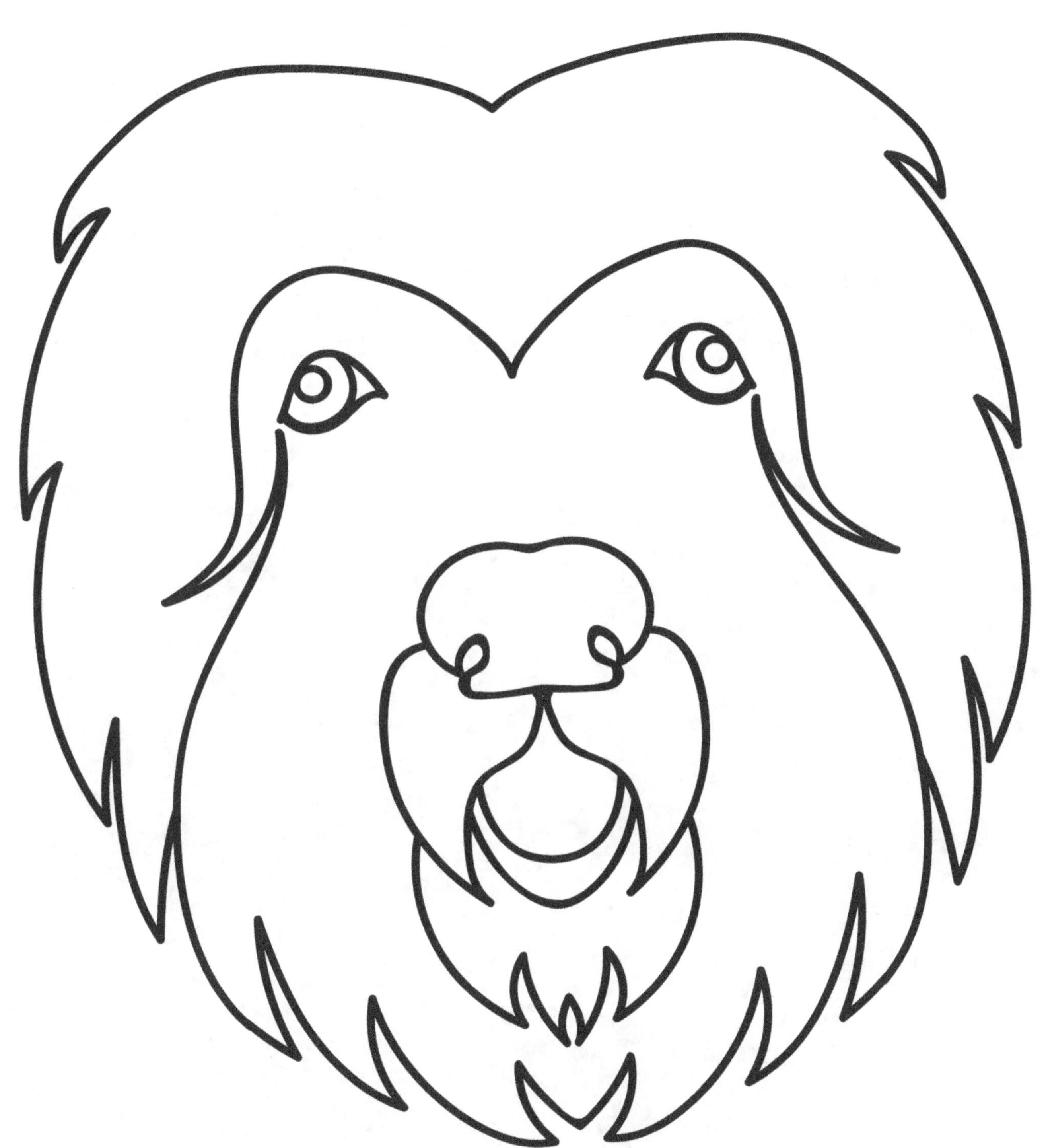

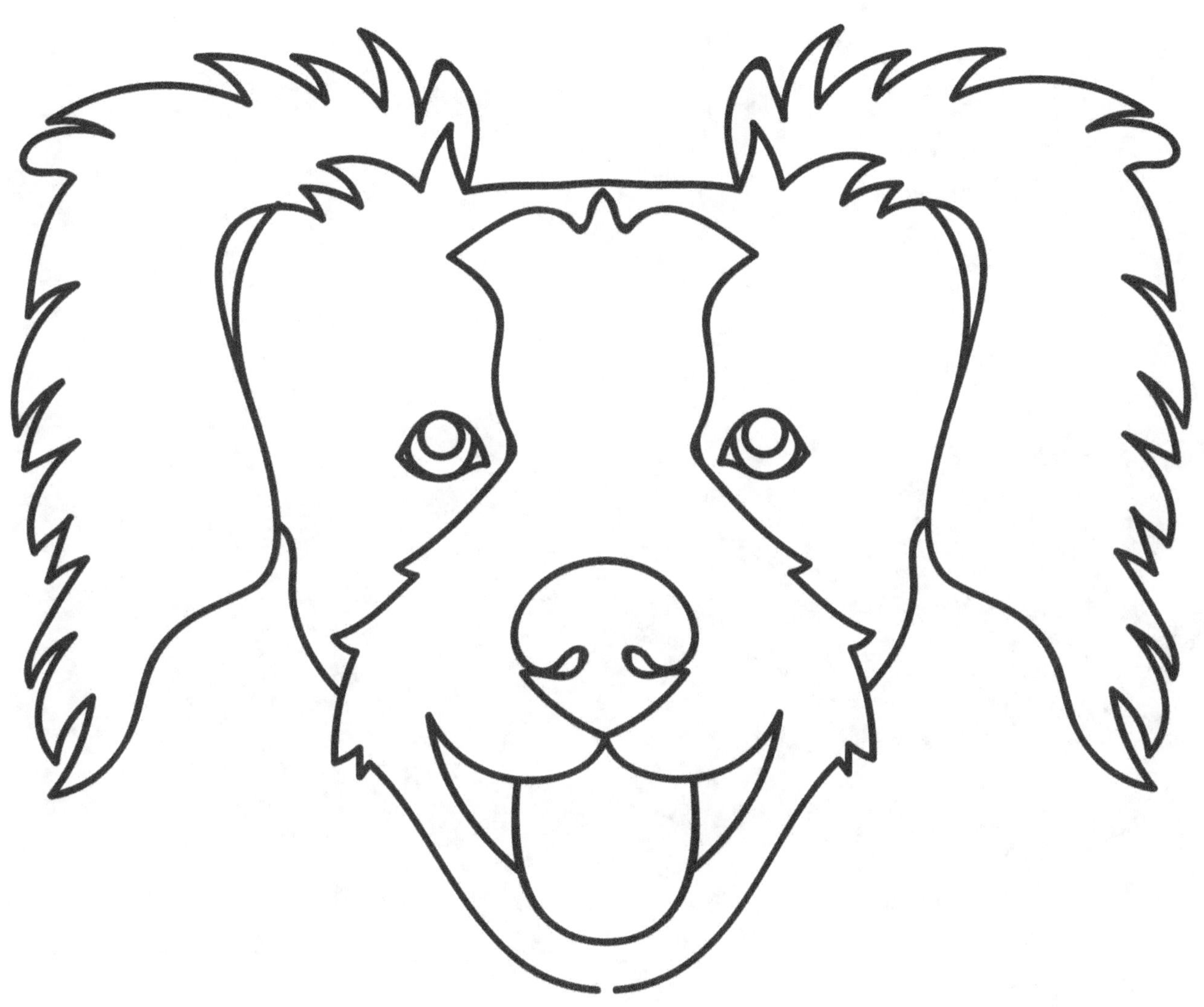

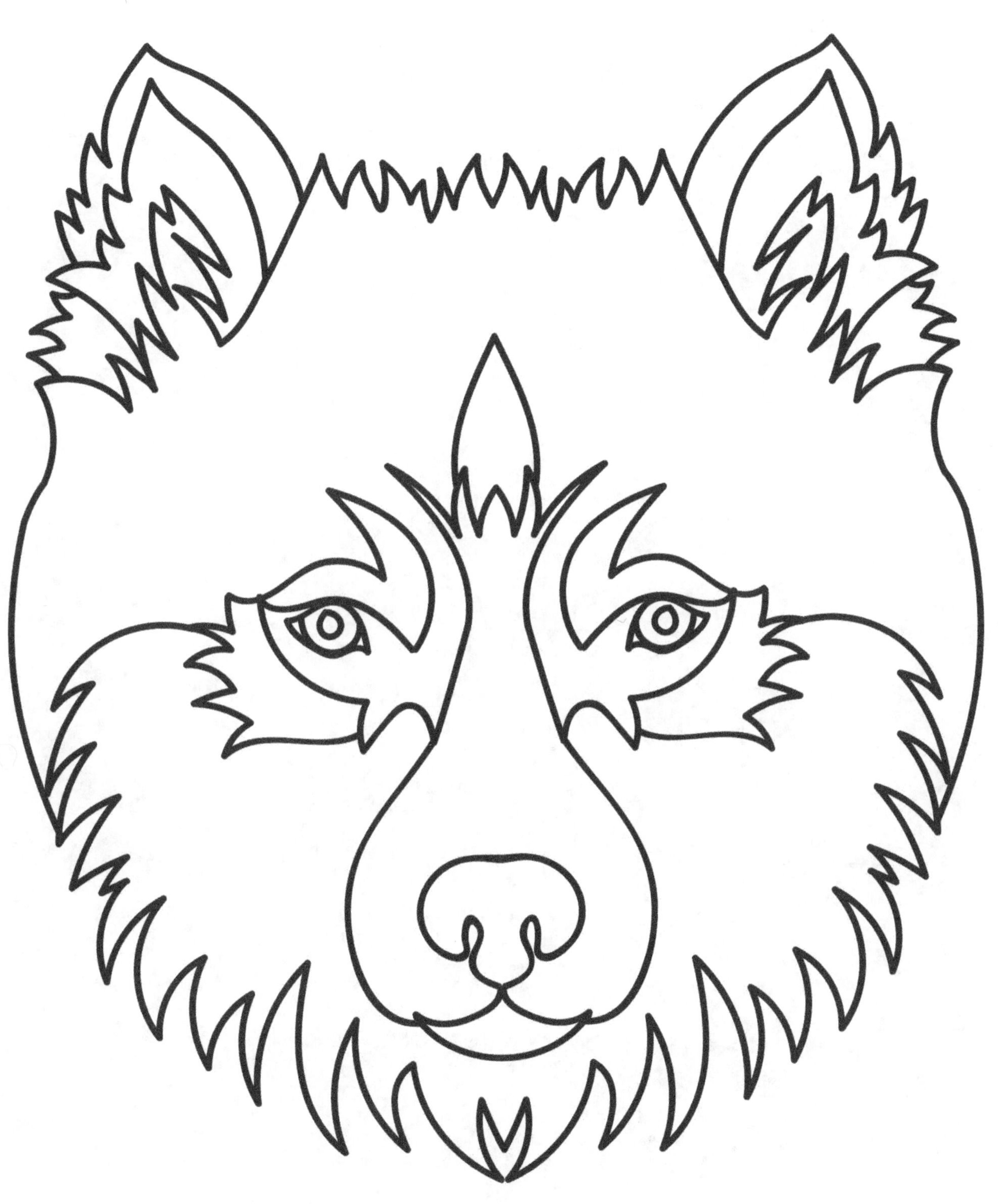

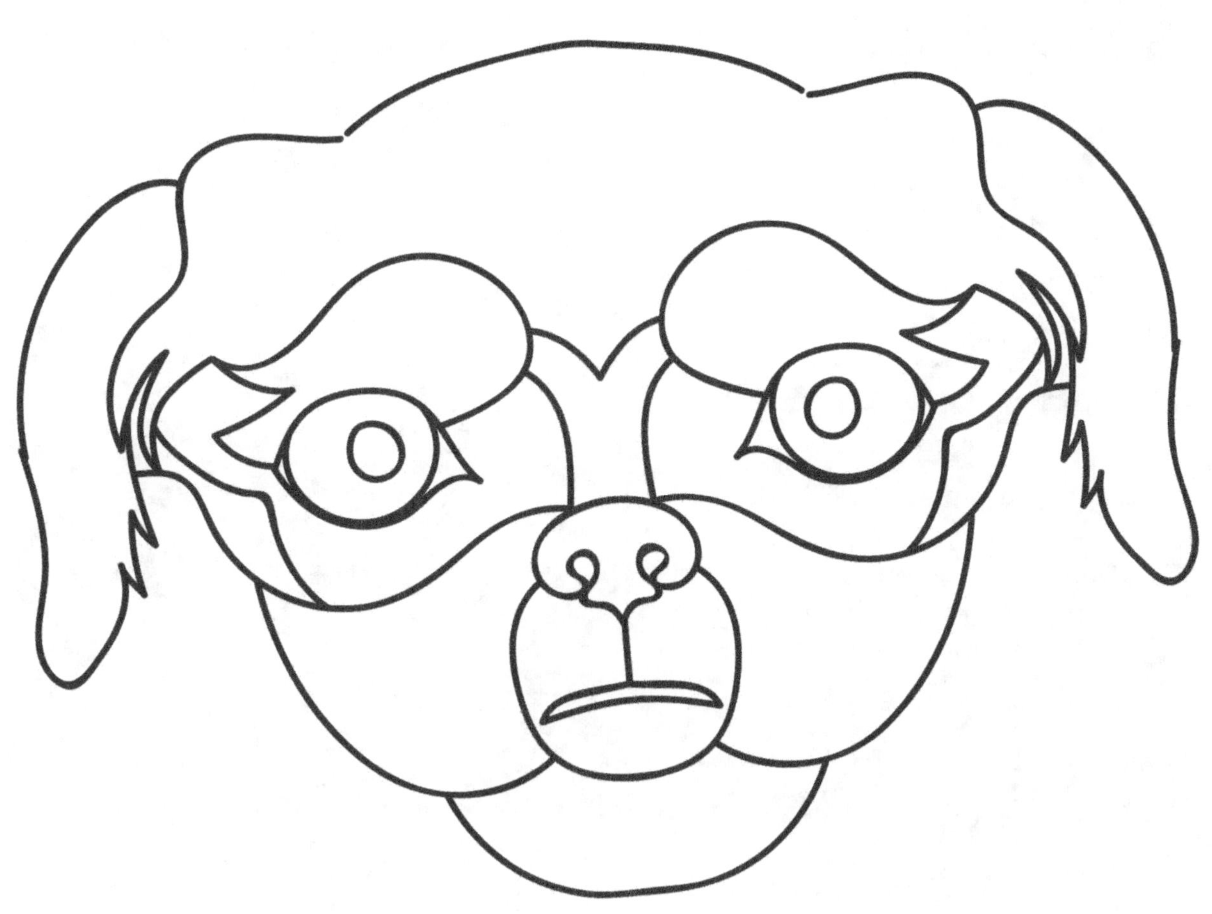

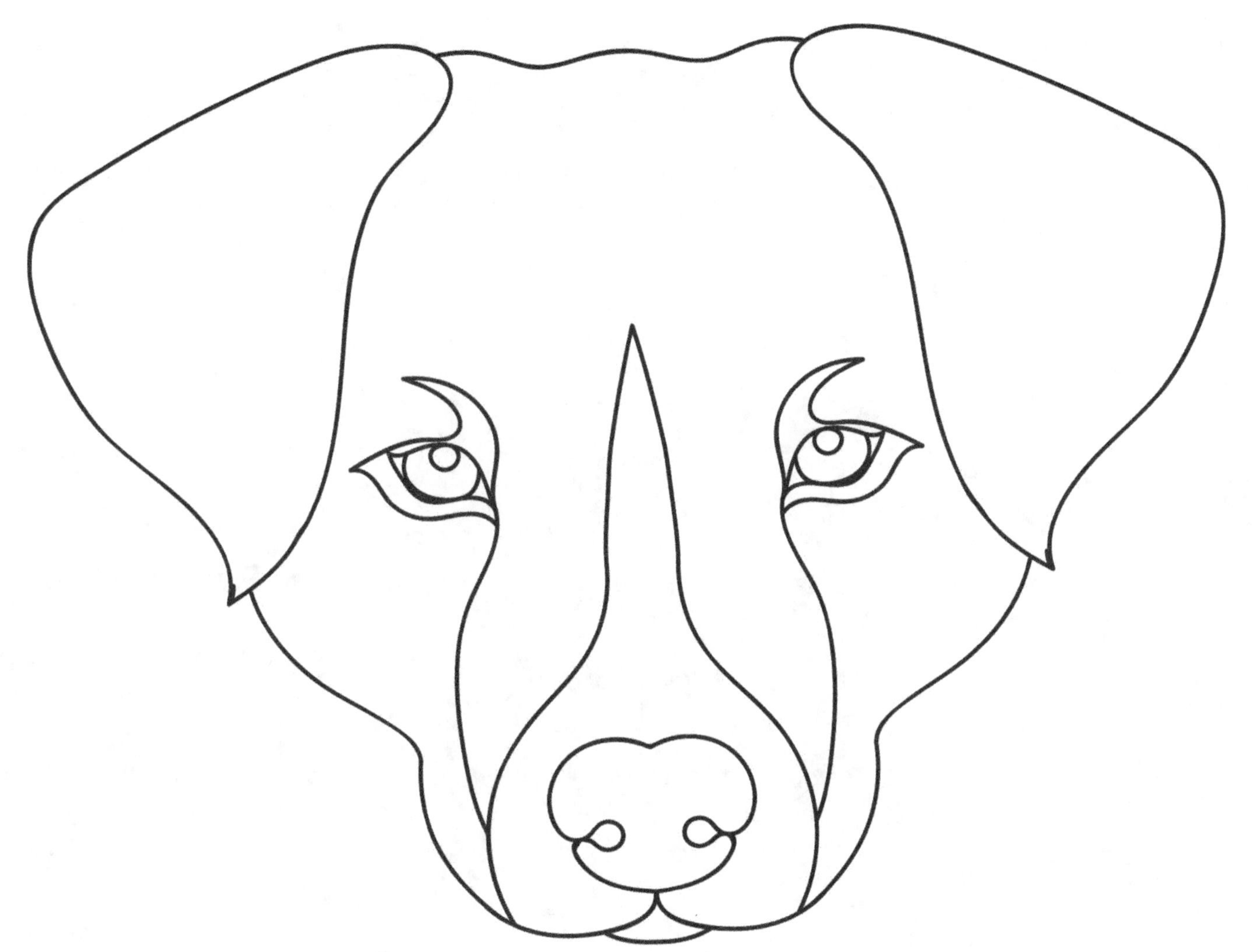

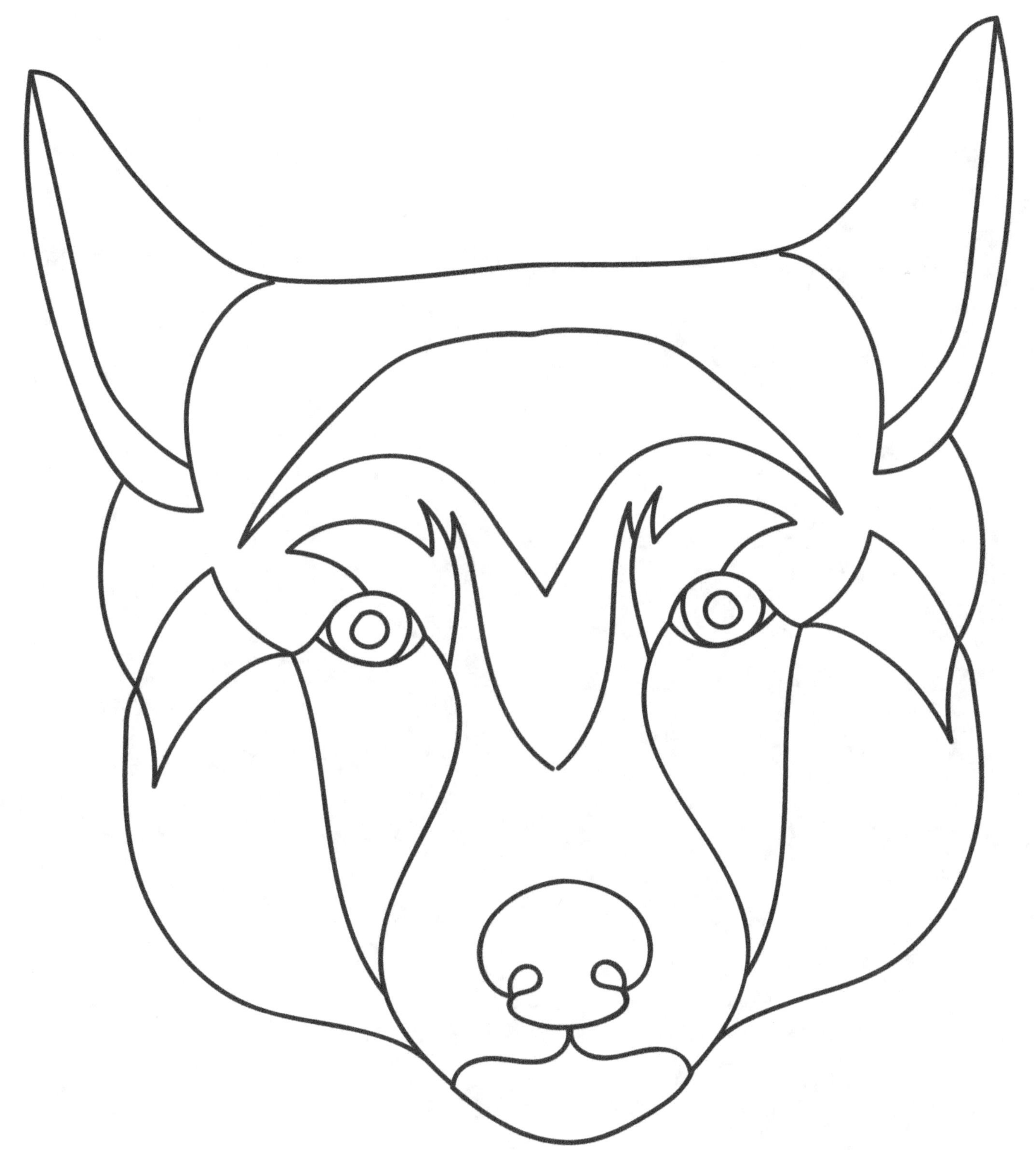

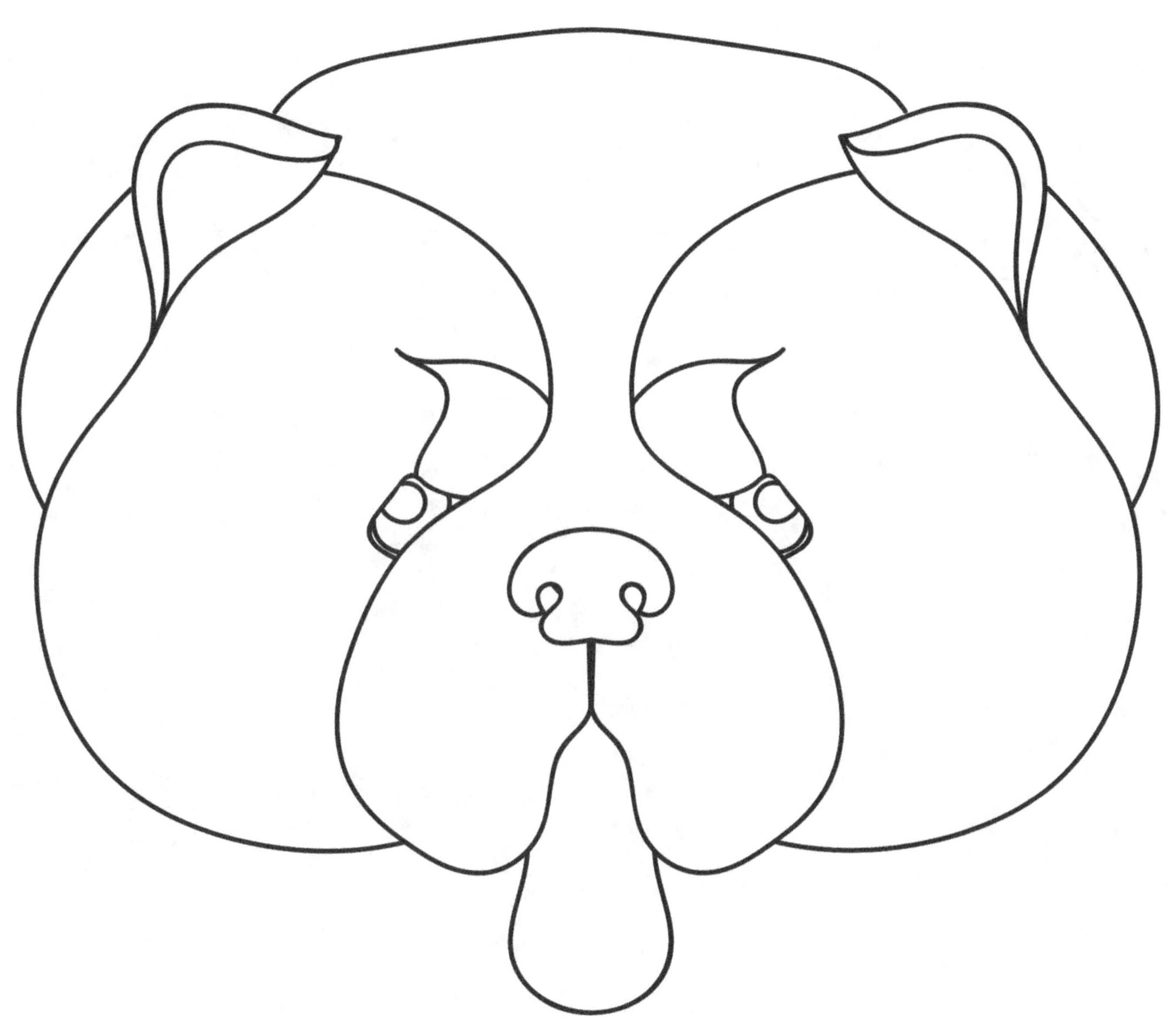

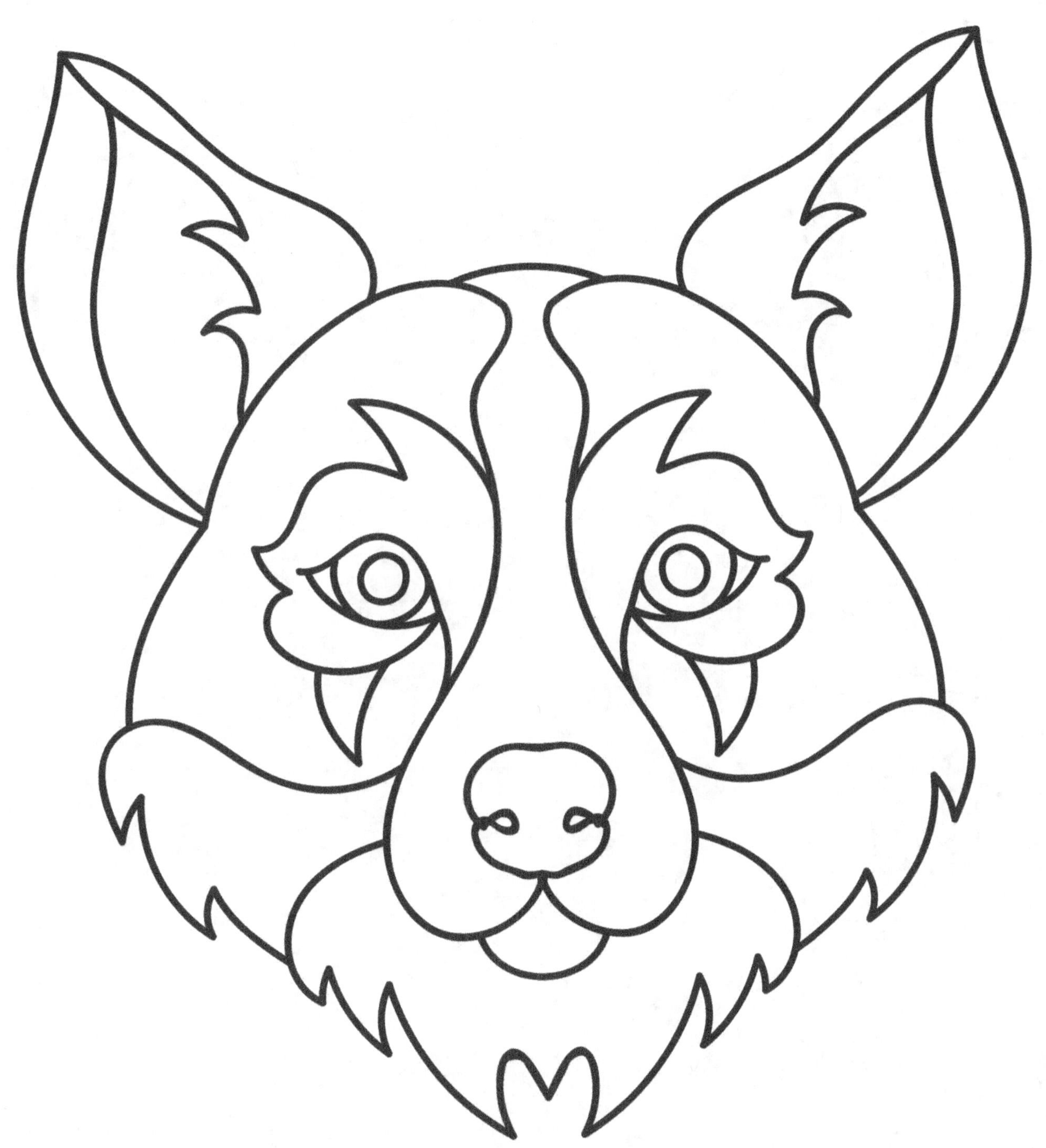

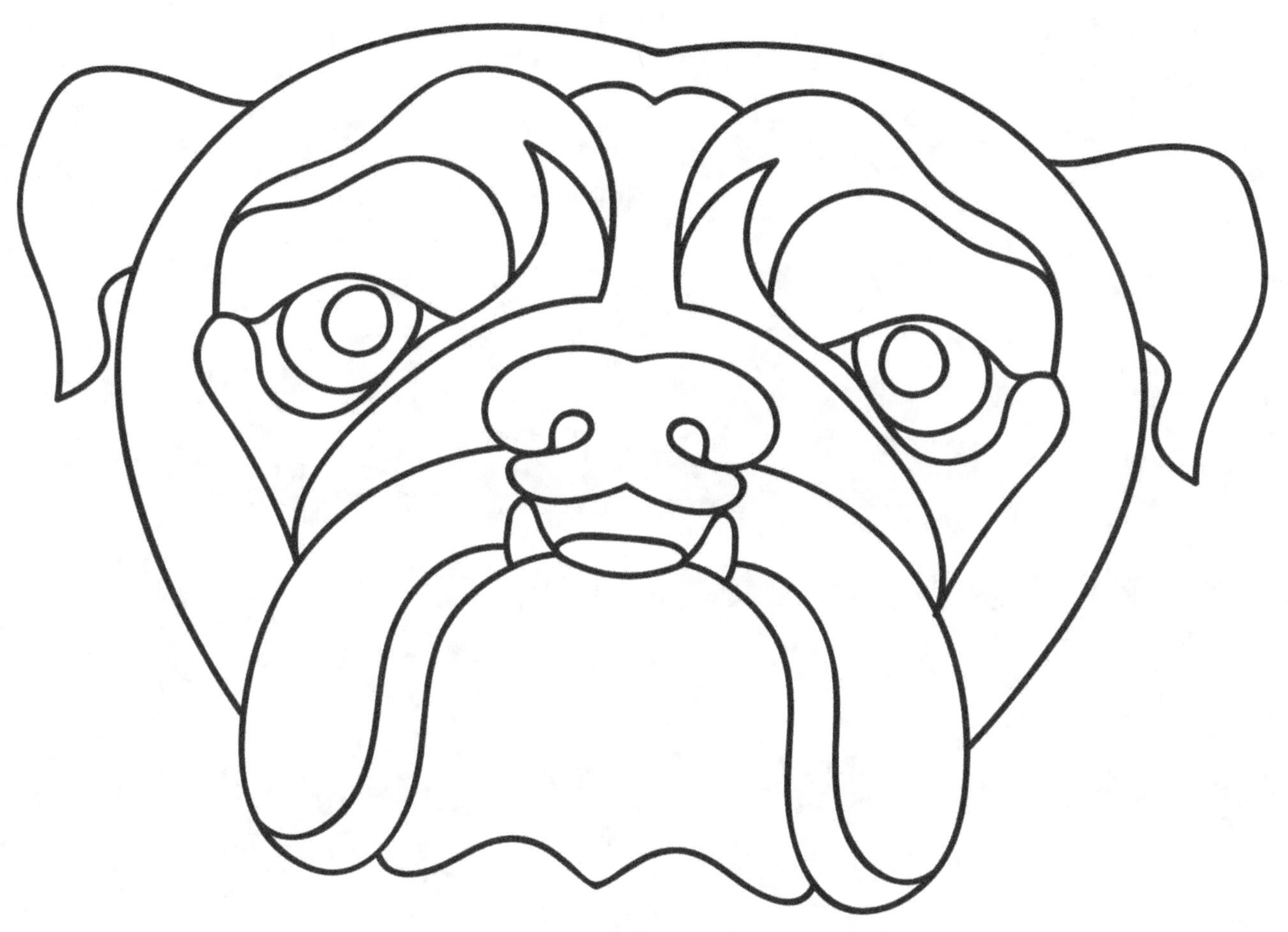

COLOR TEST PAGE

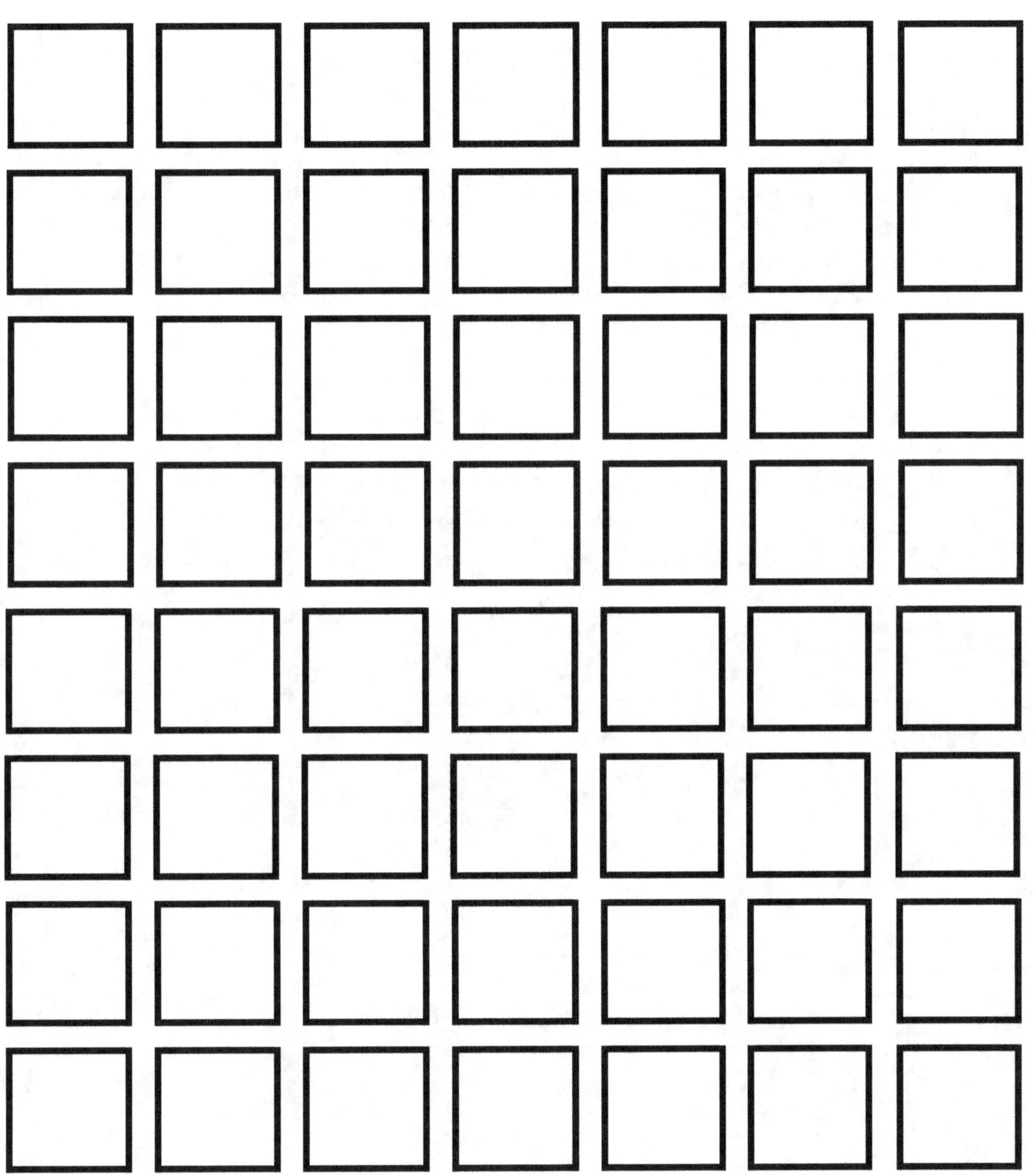

COLOR TEST PAGE